How to Talk to Little Kids With Love and Intention

An Intentional and Practical

Guide of Mindful

Communication Skills With

Positive Discipline Techniques

for Raising Kids You Actually

Like

Larry Roy Olson

professional before attempting any techniques outlined in this book.

By reading this document, the reader agrees that under no circumstances is the author responsible for any losses, direct or indirect, that are incurred because of the use of the information contained within this document, including, but not limited to, errors, omissions, or inaccuracies.

Table of Contents

iv

Your Free Gift

As a way of saying thanks for your purchases, I'm offering the book, "***Child Safety Online***" for **FREE** to my readers.

To get instant access just go to:

https://larryolson.zenserenitybooks.com/Larry-free-gift

OR

Scan this code:

Inside the book you will discover:

- *The many ways your child could be accessing dangerous sites other than on the home computer,*
- *Never to post personal information online and why,*
- *Why it's not a good idea for your child to upload photographs of themselves for strangers to see online.*

If you want to keep your child safe while online, make sure to grab the free book!

Introduction

How hard can raising a child be? I mean, they are young, easy to influence, and need our guidance to even frame the world around them, right? How hard could it really be? They are not smart, they do not really know anything—you are the one in control, you are calling all the shots. Unless, of course, you have a child and find out the reality is not that simple.

This was my experience. I thought I could wing raising my child, but I could not have been more wrong. Kids are way smarter than we think; their minds might not be calibrated for the world we live in, but they have a way of navigating through life that is profound and unbelievably impactful. They have their own communication methods, almost like a language of their own, and one that is very powerful.

In fact, there are things that kids can do way better than you can, like reading emotions and intentions in some cases. They have a way of understanding what you do and say that is completely different from how adults would, leaving a huge game between how you might communicate with a grown-up and how you might communicate with your child.

So, creating strong and healthy connections with your child is not easy; it takes work, and it takes some level of intentionality. But you know that—you have taken the first step along that journey by reading this book, and I know that this effort will pay off in the end. You really deserve to have the type of relationship you want with your child, and through the lessons in this book, you will get there.

Children are very smart; they know exactly what they are doing, and they also know what you are doing. Because they do not yet understand the world, they rely on understanding emotions and picking up the cues you show to know if they are safe or not. This gives them a heightened ability to read and understand emotions that the average grown-up does not have. They can tell when you care about them, and they can tell when you are going through the motions.

It, therefore, becomes imperative that you learn how to be intentional in how you talk to your child; especially the emotions you carry in your tone and words. If you fail to connect your communication to the emotions you want your child to feel, then you will lose the battle before it even starts. You will fail to have a good relationship with the child now, and that will compound as they grow up into an even worse relationship.

In this book, we are going to go over how the child's mind works and link that to how you can improve your communication with them to reinforce care, love, and protection. I have learned through my experiences as a parent and through those of the many other parents I have helped to improve their communication, so many things that will transform your relationship with your child.

I even remember how I got started on this journey. I had gone to visit my sister while her husband was in hospital after a bad car crash. During the week I was there, I would help with her 4-year-old every now and then as she had to juggle between work and frequent hospital visits. About a week into the visit, she sat me down and asked how I did it. I had no idea what she was talking about, and then she explained how she noticed I had been able to create such a good relationship with her child, and it was almost as if we spoke the same language.

I told her how it was not always like that; I had gone through so much trying to learn how to talk to children with compassion and love to build those connections. It had almost been too late before I learned the skill with my own child, but I was able to recreate that connection and sustain it. It was from those lessons that I learned to connect and talk to children in their language.

My sister's child was the problem, or so she thought. To be fair, when you and your child are not speaking the same language, you will have some inevitable problems. It is like meeting someone who speaks a different language, but you do not even realize it and keep insisting on using your language throughout the conversation. That is what my sister had been doing, and it did not do anything for her relationship with her child.

After I walked her through the things I had learned, she was able to drastically improve her communication and relationship with her daughter. They went from having mood swings and fighting all day long to long, sweet conversations about whether the moon was a pizza that someone left out in space to dry up. It is precious to witness, and it really made me wish I could share these solutions with more people. I am glad I have been able to—over the years, I have researched more on how the parent-child connection works and how we can better understand and talk to our children for improved connection and relationships.

I am glad I have already gotten to help so many people build their relationships with their kids and that you can benefit from mine and the tens of other relationships that have inspired this book. I know you cannot wait to get in and start learning how to talk to your child, so let us prepare to get started.

You will not need much for this journey; you already have one of the requirements—the willingness to learn. You will need to also commit to everything in the book and follow the challenges and exercises that I will leave for you throughout. I do advise you to keep a journal, especially for this journey, where you can record what you learn and your experiences as you go.

How about making your first journal entry before we move on to Chapter One? I want you to describe what your relationship with your child is like right now. Do you feel like you can understand what they are saying when they try to communicate with you? Can you tell how they are feeling, or can you hear when they do not use words to talk to you? Do you think they can hear you when you speak to them? Answer all of these and add anything else you think you might need to for the first entry in your journal. When you are done, you can join me in Chapter One as we discuss the very basis of the connection you are going to have with your child.

Chapter 1: Building a Strong Connection

So, what is the first thing you need to look at as you venture to improve your communication with your child? It is obvious what you say and how you say it is the most important thing, and that's right, but before we even get into that conversation there is something we need to establish first: connection.

Think of it this way: you pick up your phone to tell a friend something important. You pull out the notes you have made for the conversation, lay them before you, and then pick up your phone to dial them. As soon as the friend picks up, you exchange greetings, and then you venture right into your story.

You nervously introduce your points at first but continue to get comfortable as you go. You get into the emotion of every point you make, raising your voice when you need to and bringing it down when you should. You pour out your heart into it—over 30 minutes of you explaining how you feel. Maybe you are apologizing, or you are the one asking for an apology. Maybe you have a secret you have been hiding, or you are just venting. It does not matter; you are pouring your heart out to someone you love.

Now imagine at the end of the call, you realize that about 30 seconds in, the call had dropped, and the line was dead for the rest of the call. You assumed your friend was listening quietly when they were already gone. It would not matter how much you said or how you said it; it would not even matter how much emotion you put into the conversation, if the person on the other end was no longer connected, you wasted your time.

It is the exact same with the relationship you want to build with your child; if you are not connected to them, nothing you say will make a whole lot of sense. All the information and exercises from this book will fail to have the intended effect if you do not invest in creating a strong connection with your child first. In this chapter, we will go over the process of creating that connection, including how you will know when you have a strong connection—one that can carry you through the rest of the journey.

The Power of Mindful Communication in Parenting

Kids are master emotion readers, in fact, they will read your emotions more than they will hear what you are saying. Because of this, they can tell when you are being intentional about something or when you are just saying or doing it. Saying or doing everything with intention is the first and best way to create a connection with your child.

Kids love attention, so when you are talking to them, they want attention more than they want the answer. If you respond without giving attention or putting your heart into the response, then you risk making the kids feel like you do not really care about them. I have spoken to so many people who wonder how their children ended up drifting away emotionally when they were always there for them.

I find this funny because the answer is always in the question. If you are mindful and paying attention to your child, it is rare that you will not notice them drift away. You will be alert and keep your eye on their faces to see the emotion your words evoke, and as soon as you see a hint of sadness, you will mind your words and rework your response.

This is why we need to stay focused and mindful. It does not really matter what you say, but what the child *hears*. If you say something, you should be mindful of how the child will hear it, and after that, watch their reaction to see if you are right. If you are off, their face will let you know, and you can pay more attention to what you say next time. When you are mindful, you have the power to control the conversation and make sure that by the end of the conversation, your child understands exactly what you want to say.

That is the goal, after all: To get your words to be a better representation of what you are trying to say, and, therefore, improve your connection to your child. Parenting is tricky and yet fun like that: You pay extra attention to every conversation, hoping you can understand where the child is coming from, and if you are lucky, sometimes, they will say the funniest things instead. Either way, you are guaranteed being mindful will help you to create strong and formidable connections with your child.

Developing a Growth Mindset for Effective Parenting

"This growth mindset is based on the belief that your basic qualities are things you can cultivate through your efforts, your strategies, and help from others" (Dweck, 2017, p. 15). I love to explain the words of Dr. Dweck and the growth mindset. When you use the growth mindset approach with your child, you go into the relationship with the belief that the child can do anything; they are not helpless, instead, they have the power to affect and control the world around them.

Taking this approach will change how you talk to the child, but most importantly, it will also affect the type of connection you have with your child. When your default belief is that your child can do anything they set their mind to, then your communication will carry that confidence, and your child will be able to pick up on it.

Now, it is easy to understand the growth mindset approach when you also understand the fixed mindset approach. These two are opposites but in a very tricky way, so much so that most people cannot tell the difference. Here is an example to illustrate the differences: You are coloring in coloring books with your child when you realize they keep coloring outside the lines, so you stop to say something and encourage them. You could either say, "It is okay, baby, coloring is not for everyone, you will find something you are good at and excel at that." Or you could say, "Well done for trying, you will do better if you keep practicing. I will do it with you if you like, and before you know it, you will do it perfectly."

While both responses sound somewhat encouraging, they have completely different effects on the child and on the outcome of your relationship with the child. The first makes the child feel like because they failed, it means they cannot do anything,

The Neurobiology of Parenting

Creating the parent-child connection is more than just establishing great communication and having a good time; it is an inbuilt neurobiological connection. Science has proven that there is a neurological connection between every child and their parents, and this connection can become stronger depending on how the parent cares for the child (Clark et al., 2021). Yes, you are wired to have a connection with your child, and they are wired to have a connection with you as well.

If it does not feel natural, then you are not doing it right because you are neurologically wired to do it. If you learn to create a connection with your child, your neurological pathways will get behind you, and do everything they can to prepare you to become a better parent. That is the goal, right? To become a great parent and raise kids that give instead of taking from the world.

There are things you can do to make this neurological bond with your child stronger, and we will go into most of those in later chapters, but right now, I need you to know that it is possible to create the relationship you want with your child, you can have the connection you never had but longed for, or you can replicate the same love that raised you up into your child's life.

I have met so many people in life who thought it was just impossible to create a connection with children and that those who claimed to have one were just the exceptions. That could not be further from the truth, you can and should create deep connections with your child. I can tell you this now, it will go a long way into their future and into yours as well.

Why Speaking Your Child's Language Seems Difficult

Now, earlier, we talked about connectivity and how you will be wasting your time if you are trying to build a relationship with your child, but the two of you are on different pages, and there is no connection. Well, sometimes you can have a hard time connecting to your child despite the effort because you speak a different language from them.

It is no secret that there is a whole different dialect that kids use, and we might never really understand where it comes from or how it works. Even past the gugu-gaga phase and into when your child is finally speaking English, there still seems to be stark differences between the language we use and that which our children speak. To bridge this, you need to find ways to understand your child and build connections beyond just talking.

Your child sees the world differently from you; they have not yet had time to develop their own filters for seeing the world, but you are different. You have seen the world already, and you have maps of meaning and motivations that you use to judge how you should act and understand information. Your child, on the other hand, does not have that same understanding and has not yet created those schemas to help them.

These differences will show and make it hard for you to understand your child's language. Speaking in your child's language is hard because you are not a child, and you should not try to be one. It is okay that you have difficulty understanding them; sometimes they literally speak using tears, sometimes using tantrums, and sometimes they will use their faces to show how they feel and leave you to decipher what is going on. This brings us back to the previous points: Be mindful of what you say and how you say it to your child. Your language is not theirs, and that counts for quite a lot toward the quality of the relationship you get to have with your child.

Understanding Child Development Milestones and Communication

The good news is it will not always be this way, as your child grows, their language will evolve more and more with each moment that passes by. The tricky part is that you cannot wait for them to speak the same language as you to try and create a good connection because it will likely be too late.

The only way you can take full advantage of this is if you dedicate time to understanding your child from the start and then grow that connection through the years. But you are already on your way there, you have already started putting in effort to understand your child, and this will pay off. Not only in the immediate success you will see but because of the quality of your relationship with your child a few years from now.

Regardless, you need to know how your child communicates and know how to speak back to them when they communicate using these different methods. We will go over just three of the ways your child is communicating with you at different levels, and this will help you to get a better picture of what to do to hear your child through the development milestones.

Connecting Beyond Words

The primary way for humans to communicate is through words, but unfortunately, your child will not be good at using those until they have grown a bit. What does this say about your communication with your child? Well, for starters, the child will do most of their communication without using words, which will invite you to do the same to some extent.

Do not get me wrong, verbal communication is the most powerful way to connect with your child, but it is not the only effective way. To be honest, alone, it falls short quite a bit. So, it is time to get to it and learn about your child's nonverbal communication.

The Art of Active Listening

Now, while we have just gone over how your child will not always use words to express themselves to you, sometimes they will, and if you are going to build the strong connection you want to, then you will need to learn to listen to them when they speak and do it well. Active listening is an art, something that most adults fail to do with each other. It becomes even more complicated when you are communicating with a child who does not even know what they are saying themselves but who can now use words to express themselves often.

So, how is this dealt with, if at all? Well, you need to learn to listen actively to your child, and I will show you how I have learned to do this in very easy and quick steps. I have seen these steps help so many people in my profession, and I am sure they will do the same for you.

Steps for Active Listening

1. Make eye contact with the child and give them all your attention so that they feel loved and cared for.
2. Lean in slightly toward them when they are speaking.
3. Nod your head to show that you are listening.
4. Paraphrase what they have said to show that you understand.
5. Ask questions to clarify anything you do not understand.
6. Avoid interrupting them.
7. Be patient and give them your full attention.

Active listening is a great way to show someone that you care about what they have to say. It can also help you to understand the speaker's point of view better.

Navigating Technology

There is obviously a new player in the parenting game since the turn of the decade: technology. In the same way that it has changed how we do virtually everything, technology has significantly changed how we connect and relate to our children. Unfortunately, there are both benefits and disadvantages to letting technology in on our parenting, and the debate on whether or not it is beneficial is far from being resolved.

What we do know, however, is that it is impossible to keep technology out of the conversation at this point. It is here, and it is here to stay. As a parent who is genuinely concerned about their child, it is up to you to navigate the parameters that govern the involvement of technology and make sure it does not ruin what you are trying to build.

The Fight for Attention

Remember, your child wants attention, they want to feel like they are connected to you and that you are taking time to be with them and connect with them. Before technology hit the scene, there was debate about whether having pets could make children feel unloved as they would be sharing attention with the pets. Now, the conversation has moved to show how parents are failing to give their children attention because they are on the internet. The phones and laptops that are making life and work easier are also making it harder to create and maintain the relationships that we want.

If you want to build a good and strong relationship with your child, then you must prioritize them over your phone. And everything else, really. This is not only for children, but I also know you would absolutely hate it if you walked into your boss's office, and they had a whole conversation with you while on the phone. That would be very disrespectful, and you would feel like they do not value you. The same goes for friendships and family relations as well, especially romantic connections.

Given this, how much more do you think this will affect a child who depends on you for all the attention and reassurance of love that they need? That can be extremely tough on a child. If your child feels like your phone, work, or anything else is more important than they are, then they will fail to create that connection with you, and everything else you say will be pearls to the pigs. This is not a lost situation, though. You have a way to make it right in a couple of ways, but before I get into this, I must say, you can use phones and other devices. This is not a call to stop using phones and technology altogether.

That being said, let us look at how you can stop yourself from blocking off the very child you are trying to make a connection with through excessive and inappropriate use of technology. I will go over just three tips, but I know these will completely transform your life.

Do Not Talk to Your Child While You Are on the Phone

Okay, so you are in the living room scrolling through social media and having a relaxing time when suddenly your child runs in to show you something they made. How do you normally respond to this? Well, some people will bring their phone down to their chest, move their eyes away to look at the child, and then go back to their phone as they give a health-hearted remark about how nice the creation looks.

This is even better than what most people do, as most will not even bother to bring the phone down, and some people might not even bat an eye to look at the child. This is a very dangerous path, because you will create a feeling of isolation to the extent that the child thinks you hate them, or they end up feeling like they are alone, and no one is supporting them. That is slightly hard to manage when you give your child such a reaction.

So, what you should do instead is put your phone down on the table or couch before you start responding. Lock the screen and put the phone away physically. Now ask them to tell you what it is again or go over the problem or whatever the reason is for coming to you. After doing this for just a few days, you will realize that your child will feel freer talking to you, and they will approach you more often than before. When they do, they will probably wait for you to put your phone down before they start to tell you why they want your attention.

Do Not Let Your Child Talk While They Are on the Phone

The habit of talking while on the phone is one that comes naturally, and that is why you need to be intentional about not doing it to your child. You might feel like you are listening while you are going through your phone or doing whatever else, but you are not. The same happens the other way around with your child as well. There will be times when they are on their tablet or phone watching their favorite cartoon and think that it is okay for them to keep doing so as you talk to them.

Besides this being a bad habit and something that will ruin your child in the long run, it is also very bad for your connection with your child. You see, one of the things that kids will develop early is understanding how to measure the right amount of attention and when to show it. When they are born, kids are hungry for attention and will do everything they can to get as much of it with no regard for the other person or what they want.

As they get older, however, your child will start to learn to frame giving attention alongside receiving it. This is the stage where it is important for you to help them to create healthy frames around connection and interaction. While this will affect your connection with them, it will also affect their connection with the other people around them when they are older. You are responsible for teaching your child to pay attention, especially in this age where technology is constantly fighting for the same attention.

Spend Time on the Phone With Your Child and Teach Them How to be Responsible

According to a survey by the U.S. nonprofit Common-Sense Media, 47% of parents in the U.S. think their kid is addicted to their mobile device (Kadane, 2019). This is a concerning statistic and one that makes it important for you to control and lead how your child uses social media.

So many people then end up going to the other extreme end, where they completely bar their children from using the internet altogether. The problem with this is that if you do not teach your children how to use technology, then they will learn from the world around them. They will teach themselves, and it will soon become a destruction that steals their attention from you.

You cannot create a connection with your child if they are already consumed by technology. You will need to make it secondary to your relationship with your child and make sure your child understands that. The best way to do this is to schedule the times that you and your child can use the internet and for what. By doing this, you make using technology something that you do together with them and not an experience that is divorced from your efforts to connect and understand them.

Show them the parts of the internet that you think are healthy and lead them down the path that you want them to go. You have a golden chance to lead the relationship you have with your children—take it.

Building connections is not easy, there will be challenges that you will feel like you cannot handle as you go, but trust me, it is never anything you really cannot get over. If you apply the knowledge of this chapter properly then you will have the base that you need to keep going and implement the rest of the book. Since we have built the foundation, let us put it to the best test: the challenges that you will meet as you try to communicate with your child in love, care, and kindness.

Chapter 2: Navigating Challenging Behaviors With Empathy

Understanding your child is the key to everything, and it is a good thing we have gone over that. Being able to communicate with your child is the beginning, though, there is still so much that still needs to happen for you to strengthen that relationship, and we are going to go over one of the remaining steps in this chapter.

The biggest thing you will need to learn to do is approach and tackle challenging behaviors with kindness and understanding. It can be very easy to be kind and loving to your child when they are behaving and doing everything you want them to. It is when they are being difficult that you need to show them you can be empathetic.

The only thing more frustrating than when a child is throwing a tantrum in public is when their parent is also throwing one right back at them. You need to learn to respond to those difficult times with the most resolve you can master, and that is what we are going to go over in this chapter. Well, we are going to start the conversation here, but that is what the rest of the book is going to be about—you learning to talk to your child with love and empathy regardless of the situation.

Let us look at how you can start this process now, but before we get started, I have a journaling prompt for you. I want you to take this journey into your own hands and apply everything that we go through as closely as you can. You are the one in control and experiencing your relationship with your child, so it is very important that you are intentional with this process.

In your journal, I want to go over how you currently handle it when your child does something you do not want them to. So, what crosses your mind first the moment they do something you do not want them to? What do you think, and how do you start to handle the situation? What is the general response when you apply your methods, and is it the response that you desire when you get into the resolution process?

Really take a moment to think these questions over and write down your responses. Writing things down will help you to understand where you are now, and this will help you to move forward faster. When you are done with this exercise, you can journey into the next session as we discuss child psychology in preparation for the solutions to handling difficult situations.

Child Psychology

Children do not think the same that we do. Their minds are completely different and process everything differently. I know you probably think of a child simply as a smaller version of an adult who thinks the same way that adults do, but on a smaller scale. That is not the case; a child is a completely different type of person, and they are very smart.

Think of it this way: The most learning that will ever happen in a person's life happens between 0 and 10 years old. This is when all the important things are learned: language, motor movements, and cognition abilities. This is such an important stage in life that if you teach a child anything at this age, they will do significantly better than people who are trying to learn something new when they have grown up. This goes for almost anything—from a different language all the way to learning a musical instrument or a sport.

The mind of a child is very seriously capable, only in a different way than the adult mind is, which calls for different ways of understanding and analyzing the child. This is why it is hard to really define and tie the loose ends on definitions and processes in child psychology. There is so much that the child psychology schools do not agree on, but what they all cannot deny is how intelligent and unique a child's mind is.

To understand and connect at an empathetic level with your child, there is not too much that you need to know about child psychology. In fact, it all boils down to three concepts that you can use as a guide for everything else: economic, cultural, and social contexts.

The economic context refers to the economic environment around the child as they grow and contributes a lot to how a child will develop their sense of confidence, entitlement, and resource management. It is generally accepted that the wealthier the environment the child grows up in, the more spoiled they are likely to turn out. This means your child will be more entitled and likely to throw tantrums when they do not get their own way.

Your duty, in such cases as the parent, is to make sure you protect the child from either extreme so that they have the confidence that they will always get what they need if they ask, but not too entitled such that they become a problem. The best way to do this is to make sure you communicate about resources with your child from a young age. They need to know and understand that they will not always get their way, but also that you will give them everything they need. We will go over how to do this in detail in a coming section, though, but you need to get the foundations for it now.

The cultural and the social contexts are very linked, and very important to understanding child psychology. The best way to understand a child is often by looking at the environment they live and play in. This is because children are like blank canvases in a way, their best skill—which they do better than grown-ups—is simulating the environment around them.

Decoding Tantrums

It would be nearly impossible to talk about navigating challenges with your child without talking about tantrums and how to deal with them. While we will delve deeper into the topic of tantrums later in the book, I want us to lay the groundwork already so that when we get to that point you know how to establish good communication to get that conversation started.

The first thing, obviously, will be to understand what tantrums really are and where they come from. A tantrum is a fit of bad temper or uncontrolled emotion, typically one that is noisy and violent. You can already begin to see that child who rolls on the ground at the mall while their parents just look around and hope no one is watching and judging them. Not all tantrums have these extravagant shows of emotion, though, sometimes it is your child just internalizing that anger and throwing themselves into a corner to let them deal with their emotions.

Now, while tantrums are often associated with young children, they can also be seen in adults now and then. In fact, they can be seen in adults quite a bit; the only difference is that adults have found other ways of throwing their tantrums. Think about it: When you stub your toe, you shout at the top of your lungs, cursing and throwing your hands around. That is a form of a fit, really; you are expressing your pain in a loud, physically expressive way. This is what it is for kids as well, tantrums are a way for them to express their deep pain and anguish.

Most adults make the mistake of thinking that tantrums are a way of getting them worked up and irritated and retaliate in that spirit. This is very dangerous, because you are making yourself the victim when you really are not. Your child is not throwing the tantrum to upset you, even if they are throwing it at you. They are just trying to express something they think they will not be able to express well otherwise. That is to say, they do not have the ability to understand and properly order their thoughts so they can articulate them—sort of how it goes when you curse after stubbing your toe, you fail to find the best way to properly articulate how you are feeling in the moment.

So, you really need to understand what your child is trying to express through the tantrums first, address that issue, and then teach them how to express themselves better for quicker and better resolutions. It is not about you; it is about the child. I always have to go over this several times with people to whom I give advice on creating healthy relationships with children. It is really not about you, it is not a personal attack, it is not a way to embrace you, and it is certainly not a way to hurt you. But we cannot get over the fact that it will likely hurt you, and you need to deal with that. The best way to do this is to deal with the tantrum itself so that it does not keep coming back every time the same situation arises.

The number one reason for tantrums is a desire to get attention. Your child wants to feel like they are loved and cared for, and since they do not know how to conceptualize those feelings, they use tantrums to express how they feel. Remember, any child's biggest needs are love and care, and they see these through the amount of attention they receive. So, when your child throws a tantrum, sometimes they are just wondering if you care about them and still love them. Not the cutest way to ask for attention and affection, but something almost every parent has to contend with, unfortunately.

In order to create and maintain that rapport and good connection when your child is throwing a tantrum, you have to catch it and place it down carefully—the tantrum, that is. To do this, you have to stay calm and give the child a space to calm down. I know so many people out there who think ignoring the tantrums is a good solution, and in some cases, it can be, but I never recommend it, and here is why.

Remember, the number one reason for the tantrum, in most cases, is attention and affection. They might want it in the form of a toy at the moment, but it is really about wanting attention and affection. Now, if you do not give them attention and instead ignore your child when they throw their tantrum, then one of three things will happen. Firstly, your child might realize that you do not like what they are doing and stop and try to speak or express themselves another way. This is the best-case scenario, but also the least likely. Remember, these are kids, you need to teach them to express themselves, so leaving them to figure it out is not a good gamble.

Secondly, the child could actually get louder and more expressive, and get as loud and disruptive as they can until they run out of energy. Well, this might work at home when no one else can hear them, but in a store, you will not have enough energy to wait for the energy reserves to eventually run out. So, this is not really a good option either.

The last, and maybe the worst, is that your child will realize that they are not able to get your attention and stop trying. This is so bad and dangerous, and it can be the start of a separated and horrible parent-child relationship. You might interpret this as good since the child no longer throws tantrums, but the truth is, the child has accepted that they will not be getting any attention from you, and they will slowly start to drift away from you.

So, the best way to deal with the tantrum is to teach the child to express themselves well. Give them attention, not the tantrum. If you are listening to your child properly and not because they are acting out, they will feel it. This is what you should, in fact, do all the time but more so when your child is throwing a tantrum. The first step is to show them that you notice that they are trying to say something to you. Go over to them and bend down so you are closer or carry them if you still can.

After showing them that you care about them and how they are feeling, show them that you do not know what they want, and you cannot help them because you simply do not understand what the issue is. This will lead them to calm down, and maybe then they will tell you what they really want clearly. Now, even if you know what they want, you should not be reactive to the tantrum, but be proactive and pretend like you have no idea what is really going on. Do these steps enough times, and soon, they will learn that throwing a tantrum is not helpful at all.

This is a long-term solution as well because what you want to do is create a connection with your child that stops you from having to deal with the same hurdles over and over again. So, while you will see little to no progress as you start to implement this, I promise that before you know it, your child will start to understand what is going on. Go ahead, give it a try. The next time your child throws a tantrum, follow these steps. Stop what you are doing and give them your undivided attention.

When they have your attention, ask them as calmly as you can what they want and how you can help them. Do not act on their behalf until they communicate calmly. As soon as they calm down, show them that you are on their side, you just need them to be a little clear and help you to understand how you can help them.

Responding, Not Reacting

Now, let us go beyond tantrums. Most of the time, when your child cries or screams, it will actually not be a tantrum. You see, children are terrible at managing their emotions, so the smallest thing can make them smile, but the smallest thing can also make them cry. They are a mixed bag trying to manage their emotions and doing a bad job as they figure it out. This means they will often fail to deal with issues and react to situations horribly.

Adults, on the other hand, have a better sense of their emotions, but are so good at matching emotions and failing to assess the situation for themselves. This is where you need to learn to manage your child's emotions and use your own to match and hopefully calm theirs. I have worked with this one lady who would cry every time their child cried about something. One time, the child was watching TV when a fly would not stop landing on its face. Out of frustration, the child started to cry and ran to the mother.

Now, instead of being calm and reassuring the child, the mother started to cry as well. Then I asked her: Would you cry if a fly kept landing on your nose? She said no. Then I asked why she was crying then, and there was dead silence. She could not answer as soon as she realized how silly it was that she was crying. I understood her, though, she was not crying because of the fly, she was crying because the child was crying. She still needed, however, to understand that the child crying was their way of dealing with the situation as a child. As an adult, you cannot mirror the actions or emotions of a child, otherwise you will start to sound and act like them.

So, instead, no matter what your child is sharing with you, keep a calm heart. I know what you are probably thinking: *Should I really act emotionless when my child is expressing their emotions to me?* No, far from it. You can express emotion, but you cannot be caught in the emotion you are expressing. You can look sad, but that does not mean being sad. So, when your child starts to cry because their doll is refusing to drink their tea, you can show sadness to relate with your child, but you do not have to feel the same way.

When you do respond to your child, where you could react emotionally and allow that to change your mood, do the opposite, and respond instead of reacting. Always stay ahead and make sure you protect your child by giving the reaction that will help them regardless of how you really feel. In some cases, you could actually be genuinely shocked and have an emotional reaction in the moment, but even then, do not let that be what shows on your face. Stay in control and respond on your own terms. Children are masters at reading emotion; you do not want to project fear or uncertainty to them, or they will take it and allow it to ruin them. But you will have a really hard time working through the emotions if you do not speak emotions very well. This is why we need to also have a conversation on embracing emotional literacy and learning to speak the great language of emotions and feelings.

Embracing Emotional Literacy

In the first chapter, we talked about how you can improve your connection with your child by learning to speak their language. Your child reads emotions and uses those to communicate more than everything else, and therefore, the best way for you to resolve conflicts with your child is through the language they hear the clearest.

When your child is talking to you, pay attention to how they position themselves, and the pitch of their voice. You will be able to easily tell if they are afraid, happy, or even just sad. You should then use this knowledge to match how you respond. You must always respond in a complementary tone so that your child knows you are on the same page with them. If they notice that you are not connected to their emotions, which happens mostly when you are preoccupied with social media or other things, then they will disconnect, and it will become hard to find a resolution with them.

You should also be able to talk about how your child feels and bring the emotions into the verbal conversation. This is a neat trick that can help you to get your child to realize that they might be acting out of emotions, and emotions can be misleading. If your child is sad, they need to learn to identify that they are sad, and they need to also know that has a bearing on how they will act. This goes back to what we said about tantrums, the child needs to know that you do not react to their emotions, but to their communication.

It is like meeting each other halfway through. You will have to learn to speak in emotions as your child learns to speak about their emotions. If you can get your child to learn to express their emotions and actually tell you how they feel, then you have already solved half of the problems that you can encounter and need to solve with your child. More than half of these problems come because of emotions, so having a strong grip on that will go a long way.

Setting Limits With Love

Once you understand your communication and emotions and have them nailed down, then there is only one more area to look at: You will now need to learn to set boundaries with your child. Now, every time people hear about boundaries, they are quick to think of separation and detachment. While unhealthy boundaries can definitely do this, if you set your boundaries right, you will end up having a longer and happier relationship with your child.

When you set boundaries in love, you are basically stopping your child from doing things that will make you dislike them and vice versa. If you realize that there are things your child does not like, you have to teach them to communicate that so that you do not end up doing those things. In the same way, you should make sure your kids do not do anything that will get you mad and angry.

The response I get most of the time I talk about this is one of denial. Most people do not think that their children can ever do anything that would make them hate them. But that is not true. If you are not careful, you can end up hating your own child or worse, resenting them. Because we are human, we can only take so much before we cannot take negativity and what we perceive as bullying from others, regardless of age. The child will not develop these habits to make you mad, but the habit might make you mad anyway, and herein lies the problem.

This idea was popularized by Dr. Jordan B. Peterson (2018), who talked about it in his book *12 Rules for Life: An Antidote to Chaos* and said do not let your child do anything that would make you hate them. Continue to build healthy boundaries, and you will realize that, at some point, you will also create a secondary boundary that goes around both you and your child. There will be things that you both do not like, and you will be united by the boundary that you both find yourselves in, but you need to be candid and have these conversations whenever you need to.

Collaborative Problem-Solving

Your child will value and prioritize the things they learn with you more than those they learn alone. They want you to always place your seal of approval on everything they do, that is why they will come to show you everything they make and invite you to do everything with them. They know what you do is important, and what you give attention to is very important. If you give them attention and do things with them, then they will feel like you really care about them, and you love them.

Speaking in love languages with your kids will go beyond what you think. It is not just saying the things you think will make them happy and reassure them; it is also all the things you do that make them feel reassured and loved. One of the things you can and should do with your child is collaborative problem-solving. You need to be involved in what they are doing and involve them in what you do.

There are a lot of ways to do this, but the most effective that I have seen, both with my kids and the people I have helped out, is the help-me-please method. This is where you create a culture of asking your child for help whenever you are doing something they can be a part of. In turn, you can encourage your kids to ask you for help when they are doing something they enjoy.

Imagine you are about to go mow the grass outside, and your child is on the sofa watching TV, you can say, "Hey, would you like to come and help me mow the lawn?" Even if your child is not old enough to do this, the fact that you asked them will add a lot to your connection and make them feel like they are part of a team. You can actually carry them on your shoulders as you mow the lawn or have them on your back telling you which way to go. Collaboration is the best way to teach your child to resolve problems with you. Now, when there is another issue that needs to be resolved, your child will not hesitate to communicate with you because they already see you as a teammate.

Now that you are better at handling the challenges that your child will bring forth with empathy and love, I want to introduce you to another concept that is crucial for your relationship. Your child will be building their self-esteem and confidence during this time of their life, and you have such a big part to play in that. Using the knowledge you now have on handling their tantrums and negative behaviors, let us help you build your child's confidence along with your relationship with them.

Chapter 3: Cultivating Self-Esteem and Confidence

The key to building self-esteem and confidence are the foundations you lay. In order for your child to become confident, they need to know that you are there supporting them and that you believe them. It is your confidence in them that will keep them going and believing in themselves. Remember, kids only have what they can pick out from the environment around them. If there is doubt and uncertainty in the people around them, especially the parents they spend so much time with, then it will be hard for them to have confidence.

It goes without saying that you cannot give what you do not have, so maybe a good place for you to start as you try to help your child build their confidence is to make sure you believe in your abilities as a parent. Most people fail to build strong principles and a strong character in their children because they do not believe in their abilities as parents, and that ends up showing and reflecting in the subconscious of the child.

Your energy is very important, and you need to make sure it is positive and confident so that your child can draw from that and build their confidence from it. You are good enough to build the relationship you want with your child. You are good enough to help your child become the upright and successful citizen you hope they become. You have a head start: You can influence your relationship with your child and plant the schemas that you want them to develop now.

You have the ability to build the seeds of confidence now and water them as your child grows. It will not be easy to build self-confidence in your child because when they go out, they will meet a world that does not believe in them. So, they really need to have a secure source of hope, someone who will believe them when no one else does.

The Role You Play

As the parent, you have to be the captain of this process. Your child will rely on you to develop themselves. You will be their place of security, affirmation, and mostly validation. Have you ever observed how whenever something happens to a child, the first thing they are going to do is run to their parents? When they are not feeling confident, they will stand behind the parent, holding on as if for dear life, because while they may not understand what is going on around them, they know their parent is there for them. They know you are there for them.

It is not easy helping a child build their self-confidence, but it is necessary. One of the biggest mistakes you can make is to enjoy being the source of security for your child so much that you do not allow them to go out and experiment in the world. If you do not allow your child to go out and find their own identity in the world, then you will risk hurting their ability to engage with the world as they get older. They will not be able to make friends at school or communicate properly because, without you, they do not have a stable sense of self.

So, essentially, your job is to act as the launch pad as well as the safety net for your child. They should feel comfortable leaving and discovering who they are but also know they can always come back to you when they feel overwhelmed. If your child does not become socialized by age 4, it might become very hard to do it later on in life. Make sure you push them out into the world (gently) and let them develop a healthy sense of self.

Praise With Purpose: Fostering Genuine Confidence

So, how do you act as a good safety net for your child? This is a very important question because your child is going to meet and bump into so many people that will confuse them. Because they do not yet have a good understanding of life, they will fail to understand what is happening and need to come home running. This is where you come in, you should be on standby, ready to hold them and reassure them.

You should be there to offer praise and give them a pat on the back for going out and trying. Praise is such a great booster for your child's confidence, it is what they use to decide two very important things: one, if they are good, and two, if they should do something again. Using praise with your child also teaches them to be proud of themselves for choosing the good thing over something else.

Let us start with the first. Your child wants to figure out if they are good at what they are trying to do. We went over this earlier when we talked about the growth mindset and your child's brain. They will come and show you what they made or what they are doing because that approval is the seal that they need to keep doing it and trying to do it better. When you praise them for doing something, they do more of it. It is funny to see sometimes. I have a 5-year-old cousin. Sometimes, when he cleans up and I say, "thank you" and praise him for it, the next thing I know, he is trying to lift the couches and clean the whole house upside down. This is typical of all children and gives you a tool that you can use to reinforce the good things your child does.

When your child does something you want them to do more of, praise them for it. This will make them feel good about it and encourage them to build self-confidence around doing that one thing. This is actually a trick you can use with grown-ups as well. People, in general, love to be praised and will do anything they think will garner them praise and admiration. If you want to reinforce a behavior, you only need to reward it, and it will persist.

I want you to start doing this now. Remember, this book is not just about the information, it is about taking action and integrating all the things that you learn into building your relationship with your child. I want you to think of something your child has done recently that you liked and praise them for it. In your praise, show that you are grateful for the effort they put in.

There is a very simple formula for praising your child that will help you to get it right every time. The format is simply, *who, what, and when.* You need to mention who did the behavior you liked first, then what that was, and lastly, when. After this, you can add that well-deserved "thank you." It might look something like this, "Linda, you cleaned the living room so well this morning. Thank you very much, I am so grateful." You can never go wrong with this method. Just make sure you always keep your tone sincere; kids can tell.

Turning Failures Into Growth Opportunities

What about when they completely fail to do what they were trying to, what do you do then? It is easier to be supportive and build self-confidence when your child is doing the right thing. All you have to do is encourage them to keep going and continue doing what they are doing; so, what do you do when they are failing to do something?

Here is what you do not want to do: Do not focus on the failure. For example, when your child tries to color and they color outside of the lines, do not focus on what they did not do right and how they are all over the page with their crayons. Instead, make a note to only look at what they did right and focus on that. It is like the glass is half full. When the child fails, no matter what it is, all they see is the failure. If they were in a race and came out in third place, all they see is that two people were faster than them, and they might miss that they were faster than seven other people.

I once read, "By using praise, you are showing your child how to think and talk positively about themselves. You're helping your child learn how to recognize when they do well and feel proud of themselves" (Raising Children Network, 2017). This, therefore, means that it is your duty as the parent to point out what the child does right and praise it. It will show them that no matter their performance, you will be there to support them, and if they try again and do better, you will praise them even more. Instead of becoming afraid to try, your child will actually become excited to do it again, even after failing.

Body Positivity and Self-Image: Nurturing a Healthy Self-Concept

Children can be ruthless without even noticing it. I have heard so many parents talk about how some other child called their child ugly at the playground. This is such a common occurrence with children because they have not yet fully developed a filter and the diplomacy that we, as adults, have. Most body image issues actually start with children when they are told they are ugly, fat, or thin by their peers. You then have the duty to speak love and beauty into that situation to counter those words out in the playground.

Children love using what their parents or teachers say as a defense against what the world teaches them. There is nothing that says I am resolute about my belief more than when a child says, "My dad said...." It becomes the law, and nothing can take that from the kid. So, think about it: If someone calls your child ugly, but they cannot recall you saying otherwise, what will their defense look like? You are the anchor for what is true in your child's life, and you should make sure you tell them what you want them to believe.

Tell your child they are good-looking at least once every day. You can do this either in the morning as you are leaving for work or as they are leaving for school. Having this as the last thing you say will make it stick out in their minds throughout the day, making it a great day for them, on top of being a confidence booster. There is a very strong correlation between self-image and how your parents talk to you, and you need to know this is the case with your child (Mental Health Foundation, 2022). You are not only helping your child in the present, but you are also helping them in their future as well. That is the point of parenting anyway, it is not just about how you help your children now, but how you help shape their future as well.

Mindful Affirmations

As we close off this chapter, I want us to look at something practical that you can both do with and teach your child—mindful affirmations. Mindful affirmations are a way to drill the truth into your child's mind so that it will challenge ideas that try to bring them down. Think of it this way: You will be able to target the areas of your child's life that make them feel insecure. If your child is having a hard time making friends, then you focus on that with the meditations. If your child is struggling with their body image, then you create affirmations that address that.

The best way to do this, therefore, is to first find out what makes your child insecure and why. The best way to do this is to use the point of negotiation that we went over earlier. Sit down with your child and have a conversation with them about life. It is during these conversations that you will realize what your child is going through, and if you fail to, you can always ask.

After you get a good look at what you are dealing with, you can have affirmations that are precise and confirm what you want your child to believe. For kids, start all the affirmations with "I am." This is a great way to frame the affirmations because the kids will easily believe the words because of their accepting minds. The following examples make good guides for affirmations: You can high-five your child every night and every morning to help their self-esteem.

- I am a superstar!
- I am super good at math!
- I am so fast on the track; I will make it!
- I am beautiful, and you can't convince me otherwise!

43

There are so many other affirmations that you can use with your child. In fact, you can, and should create rotating affirmations for what your child needs the most in each situation. Do not make it a tiring process, add high-fives and some team spirit into the affirmations. Make them into something your child will remember and also enjoy.

There is no need to wait, go and do this now. You are responsible for your child's self-image, and that is something that you need to always take seriously. Your words are law to your child, if you tell them they cannot do something, then they will really think that they cannot, and if you tell them they can do it, then they absolutely will. Do not take for granted the power of your influence in both the life of your child and the quality of the relationship you will end up having with them. Knowing this, let us look at how you strengthen the relationship even more through cooperation and mutual respect.

Chapter 4: Fostering Cooperation and Mutual Respect

Your kids are your partners, and they want to feel like that. I have realized that one of the biggest mistakes you can make as a parent is thinking that your children are nothing more than helpless little humans that you are supposed to love and care for as long as you can. You are supposed to love and care for your children as much as you can, but your relationship with them is more complex than that.

Being the first human they have contact with, your child will probably create a connection with you to fulfill more than one role in their life. You will be their friend and partner. Children love feeling like they are an important part of the family and that you actually value them as such. This is how you foster cooperation and mutual respect between yourself and the child.

I love it when I sometimes call my kids for a meeting and talk to them like they are actual stakeholders in the house. It could be something as simple as asking them what they want for dinner all the way up to negotiating what you are going to buy for them for their birthday. It is so much fun for you and really helpful for your child's development because you really need to learn how to develop your child's sense of cooperation and respect. Let us go into how you can do this without taking all the fun out of parenting and ruining the connection you have built with your child so far.

Finding Win-Win Solutions With Kids

The first thing you will need to do is have conversations with your child and try to teach them to negotiate. Negotiating with your child is about having win-win solutions every time there is a decision to be made, and there will be so many to be made. I want you to see your child as someone you want to build a relationship with that lasts to the end of time. This will change how you deal with negotiations with your child.

I know so many parents who are on a yes or no basis with their kids, and this is so bad for the connection you are trying to build. Imagine this from a different perspective: If every time you asked for something from your partner or your boss, they just said no or okay. No explanation, just an agreement or disagreement. That would make you feel like it does not matter what you think, and if they want something to happen, it will, but if they do not, then it will not (Gallo, 2023).

This is the same with your child. Even when you want to say yes, allow them a chance to feel like they deserve the yes, like they presented a good case. When you are saying no, explain why you are saying no to your child. They need to also know that you listened to what they said, but you just cannot give them what they want right then. This is what negotiation is. You can even counter offers and allow your child to counter as well. If you do this, you raise a child who knows how to deal fairly and communicate with others in the world.

I try this trick with my kids, and it works so well: Every time they ask me for something I cannot or do not think I should give to them, I always give them an alternative. I will say something like, "We cannot get ice cream right now because we are late to pick up Mommy from the airport, however, when we get home, I will help you ask Mommy for some of her white chocolate." This will make the kids feel that I am actually concerned about their request, and I will help them to get something that still fulfills them.

Be in the habit of negotiating with your children. As I said, they might not be as smart as we are, but kids have their own unique way of seeing the world, and they are not dumb. So, it is not really about whether you say yes or you say no. The real problem is how you do it. If you do it with respect, then you are likely going to strengthen the relationship regardless of what you say.

The Power of Choice: Empowering Your Child in Decision-Making

Now, it is not always that you need to negotiate with your child; sometimes, let them make the decision and give them options to pick from. You will be the final decision maker in most of the cases, so it will be really good if you can give your child the opportunity to do the same every now and then. You will have to set some control, of course. You cannot allow your children to pick anything for dinner, or it will end up being cookies and juice with chocolates and ice cream. However, you can ask your kids if they want to go out or eat in.

The real idea is for you to allow your child to make good decisions. Every time they pick something, they are giving up on another option, and this is a very important lesson to share with your child. I am challenging you to start this today. Go to your child and ask them what they want for dinner, and give them three options. The first thing you will see is a big smile on their face as they realize they have just been given power and the opportunity to make a decision.

Once you start doing this, your child will start to respect you a little more, but more than that, they will also start to respect themselves more. Your kids are going to realize that you think they can make decisions, and that will bring them to a place of embracing it quickly and becoming a better person.

Teamwork at Home: Creating a Cooperative Environment

The question you should be trying to answer is, how do I create a collaborative environment at home? While it would be great to involve your child in the things you do every now and then, it would be way better if you could create an environment that makes that an everyday thing.

Children are impacted by routines way more than adults, which means if you have them do something consistently, then they will get in the habit of doing that thing all the time. The best way to get a habit started with your child, is to have routines that have them doing that same thing often throughout the week. So, I want you to think about what you can do together with your child every week, what your child can do that you can help them with, and what you can do that your child can help you with.

Once you have these figured out, make a schedule, and have it on the fridge or in a spot where you both can see it. This will be a constant reminder that there are these collaborative activities that you both need to do. Now, I know most families are bigger than just you and your child, and if that is the case with you, then I encourage you to get the rest of the family involved in the plans as well. Get an activity that you do as a family, another that the kids do alone, and maybe another that the adults do on their own. This idea of building recurring activities that are on everyone's schedule, forces all of you to work together at least once every week, and this will impact your relationship strongly.

Encouraging Independence

I know we have been focusing on working together and building cooperation with your child, but we also need to talk about the opposite of that—encouraging independence. You see, while it is great that you can build a strong team ethic with your family, it is also important that you raise a child that has the ability to build a life independent of you and of the rest of the world.

So many people get lost in trying to make their children a part of their life, but they can do so much that they will eventually swallow up their children's lives and leave them completely dependent on them. That is not the goal here, that is not what we are going for at all. You have to teach your child to be independent, and you have to show them that it is because they are a different person with distinct skills that you like to work with them.

This is best done verbally by telling your child how they are unique and how they contribute something to the world. Instead of just asking them to help you cook, say something like, "I know you are good at this, maybe even better than me at some stuff, come and help me cook. I will not do as good of a job without you." This makes the child feel that they are there to help because they are worth something and they can actually do something.

To add to that, encourage them to go out and do other things even when they are away from you. Ask them about what they have done when they were away from you. When your child knows you are going to ask them about how their day was and talk about what they did, then they will do as much as they can throughout the day because they want to tell you about it when the day ends.

Train your child for flight. It can be tempting when you are trying to build a connection with your child that you build a relationship that keeps other people out. You might want to keep your relationship strong by keeping your child dependent on you, and this works, but it will not serve you very well. I want you to go ahead and think about how you will encourage your child to go out in the world and become everything they are supposed to be. Let them fly—seeing them soar is part of the joy of being a parent.

Sibling Relationships

Sibling relationships are super complicated. Siblings will refuse to share a phone charger, but willingly give away a kidney to the other if they need it. They will make fun of each other relentlessly but will not take it well when someone else does the same. They are special relationships that are hard to manage as a parent. You need to give sibling relationships space and time to develop on their own but make sure you pay attention to how things are going so that you can ensure everything is okay and a good relationship develops.

I advise that you always look at your relationships with your kids individually rather than as a group. You cannot give your children the same type of attention all the time because they are different, and they have different challenges in life. You need to figure out what each child wants and then customize your interaction, cooperation, and attention to them to fulfill that need. Earlier, we talked about building custom affirmations for your child so that you can target what they are going through. If you have more than one child, then make sure you do this for each individually and privately. Show them that you care about them as an individual.

However, you should create situations that teach the kids to interact every now and then. I have what I call the two-at-a-time rule. Every time I want something done, I will ask the kids to do it together, even if it only needs one person to get it done. This means they will have to communicate and negotiate who is going to do what and when and how. This will easily and seamlessly teach them to work together and build the relationship you want to see among your kids.

Now, remember, your child is also your partner. They are not just a child that you have to take care of, they are an important part of your life that you consult and talk to about things. You allow them to make decisions, especially when it comes to areas that concern them. This is a very powerful tool if you want to raise your child as a strong and independent individual.

The journey does not end there, though, in addition to what you have learned, you need to add a few more ideas and concepts. You see, these ideas are not just information. The idea is to do everything you can to bring them into your life and see results. I do not want you to just read through and then go back to struggling to communicate and create a good connection with your child. Remember, you deserve to have the relationship with your child that you are aiming for. You can have it, and you deserve it.

Now, let us move on and see how you can still remain the voice of discipline to your child without pushing them away. This is one of the hardest things to do, but you have the strength and wisdom to handle it well.

Chapter 5: Disciplining With Love

Disciplining has evolved so much over the years. We went from a time when children would get whipped and hit with rods all the way to now when some people do not even think that children should be disciplined. The truth is, if you do not discipline your children, the state will do it for you later. Which do you prefer: having the state take your child when they are grown up, and taking them to their institutions, or spending time now to discipline them yourself?

The correctional facilities that the state has in place are the last resort to curbing the bad behavior that you might have had a chance to take care of while your child was still young. So, in this chapter, we are going to look at how you can discipline your child in a way that gets rid of the bad habits and behaviors and not the child.

I have seen so many people struggle with their children because they do not discipline them well. It is a very thin line between too much and too little discipline. If you are not careful and intentional, you will end up on either side of the line, and that will not be good for your child and for the connection you have with your child.

The Mindful Discipline Approach

Mindful discipline entails one thing above all: You are mindful of how your child is affected by the method of discipline (Shapiro & White, 2014). It is not about how you discipline the child, it is more about how your child will be affected by it that matters the most. So, the most important question when you are about to decide how to discipline your child is, how will this make them feel?

Imagine this: You are disciplining your child for spilling milk all over the kitchen floor while they are helping you make some muffins. You warn them one time, but after a while, they are pouring the milk on the ground again, what do you do? You could take it away from them and send them out of the kitchen and tell them they cannot help you anymore. That option sounds okay, right? You were not harsh, and you also solved the problem by getting them out of the kitchen. Or did you?

You might have taken them from the space that allowed them to do the wrong that they did, but that does not mean that they will not do what they did again if they are in this situation in the future. So, you did not help your child to stop doing the negative behavior in the long run. In fact, you have

56

made the child feel like they are useless in the kitchen and that they cannot do anything helpful.

So, what could you have done instead? Well, let us go through the principles of mindful discipline and see how you can handle this situation better. The general idea is to teach your child to behave differently next time in the clearest way possible. You are not here to inflict pain on them, but rather to lead them.

Be Present and Engaged When You Are Disciplining Your Child

I cannot say this enough: You need to be there and give your child attention. We talked about how paying attention when you are listening to your child will help you to get through better, and this is no exception. You need to take time to engage in the situation and make sure your mind is present as well. Because of this, you do not even have to always deal with every issue immediately, you can make sure it is the right time first.

Focus on the Behavior, Not the Child

Now, I want you to focus on the issue and not the person who did the action. This is important because it is the difference between helping a good child who did something bad and punishing a bad kid who did something bad. You should see the action as it is: irresponsible, mischievous, bad, and harmful, but keep those descriptions from the child. If you do this, then you will still be able to give the child love and care even through this process.

Explain Why the Behavior Is Wrong and What the Consequences Will Be

Now, you should explain what the child did wrong. Imagine it like there are three people in a negotiation: you, your child, and the action itself. When you start to talk to your child, you are on one side while your child and the action are on the same side. Your job during this step is to convince the child that action is bad and show them why. If you do this well, by the end, your child will be on your side, and you will both be looking at the behavior as the enemy.

Now, this is also the stage where you address how there are consequences for what the child did. I want you to split this into two categories: the consequences to you or the people around the child, and then to the child. Here is how that looks when we look at the example with the child pouring milk on the ground. You can express how you might not be able to make enough muffins for everyone because you will not have enough milk. Show how this will affect other people in the house who will not be able to have muffins anymore. Now explain that because of this, you are going to miss out on their amazing help in the kitchen because you have to send them away.

Give Your Child a Chance to Apologize and Make Amends

Now, you do not just say this and then send them out of the room. You give them a chance to respond and show that they have understood what you are saying and why you are saying it. This will look something like asking them what they think or just being quiet and waiting for them to say something. Once your kid says they are sorry, it is time to ask them how they will do it next time or how they can fix it. In this case, they can offer to wipe the milk they split and make a promise not to do it again. When this happens, you can take away the punishment and allow them to clean up. You can even help them with the clean-up to show that you are on their side and that you still love and care about them.

Remember That You Are Teaching Your Child, Not Punishing Them

In all of this, the most important part is remembering that you are teaching and training your child and not punishing them. You are going to have to be patient, explain, and listen to your child to achieve this. The best part is that it is usually the intention that changes the outcome. In the initial example, we went through something that felt very similar to this, the only difference was the intention and the way you spoke to the child.

Now, you will need to be clear and figure out when and how you can use these tips. You are not supposed to just do this in the same way every time, but you should understand what the guiding principles are and allow those to become a part of how you deal with your child. You might not have the time to grab the book and read these steps every time you have to discipline your child, but you can start using these principles now and allow them to guide you.

Mindful discipline can be a challenging but rewarding way to raise children. It can help children to learn from their mistakes and develop into responsible, respectful adults instead of creating a rift unnecessarily between you and your children.

Shifting Focus From Negative to Positive

Now, let us talk about an element in the previous session that you need to hone in on if you are going to be effective at disciplining your child. Whenever your child does something wrong, there are two sides to that action, it is wrong because there is something right that should have been done instead of the wrong thing that happened. So, you can look at every situation as a measure of right and wrong. Your child should understand that the goal is to do right as much as they can and that you are there to help them do that.

This is why you discipline them in the first place, you want them to learn to do good and become good, even if it is just for their own benefit. If your child understands this, then they will not see it as a need for you to just have everything done your way, but instead, because you want them to grow and develop for their own benefit instead. You will realize that kids can tell when you want them to behave well for your own benefit, maybe for your image in front of your friends, or so you do not have to do a lot of parenting. You want to avoid doing this by focusing as much as you can on the child and how they can do better if they handle the situation better next time.

This means that when you are teaching your child after an incident, you should be focusing on what they should do right next time and what the good is that they missed. Instead of pounding on what was done wrong, look at what they could have done right and how that would have been helpful for them and not just for you. This is how you divert from all of those accusing and blaming statements: "You split the milk, you lost the money, you did this, and you did that." Saying these accusing statements will only make your child feel guilty and shameful, and that will not help either you or them.

When they feel like they could not have done better anyway because, like you would have said using those statements, they are unable to and can only do what is wrong, then they will not even try to improve for next time. Your words during discipline are so important, and while it is important to show that you are disappointed, you want to try and show it in a positive light.

Instead of saying you are sad that they spilled the milk, say you are sad that it is going to take time to clean it up, and that affects your time together and how the muffins will come out eventually. Talk about the good that should have happened, and that should still happen. When the child walks away from this situation, they will think to themself, *my mom/dad does love spending time with me*, and if anything ruins that, they get sad.

Imagine the alternative: They can walk away thinking, *my parents do not like me because I spilled the milk, my parents do not like me because I am clumsy*, or even *my parents do not like it when I ruin their things and would prefer I stay away when they are doing stuff*. Yes, children think like that; they are not adults, and their brains, special and effective as they are, cannot work as effectively as ours do.

So, they work based on emotion. If they sense rejection in your tone, then guess what you are communicating? Rejection. If they hear separation in your tone or disappointment, then that is what you are communicating. This is why you need to be mindful and take your time to think about what you are going to say and how you are going to say it.

Time-In Instead of Time-Out

Another strategy I want you to seriously consider is time-in instead of time-out. I learned this trick from a friend when I was talking to him about how I always felt time-out was not very effective. Think about it: Time out is all about isolating your child from the rest of the world and leaving them to their emotions and thoughts. This might not be the best idea at all.

Think back to when you were still a child; when you went into time-out, did you really think about reconciling your thoughts to your parents or just how much you hated them for putting you in time-out? Even though the child's mind is super complex and able to do so much, part of what it cannot do is self-calibrate. This means when you put a child in time out, you are leaving them with their young mind to figure out answers that they cannot really come up with.

Time out does not work because the child realizes how wrong they were or understands what they did wrong. Time-out only works because the child feels isolated, and they will do anything to be able to come back into the embrace and comfort of the people around them.

So, this is where the better solution comes in: time-in. Instead of pushing your child away and leaving them to the devices of their own mind, you can pull them in and help them to think through it in the comfort of your reassurance and your love. You can say, "Okay, it is time for a time-in. Come, let us talk about it. What happened is not right, and we need to address it." Give them a big hug and start trying to reconcile and figure out why they acted as they did together (Heid, 2019).

In addition to being a better solution, this will also help you to establish yourself as the person that your child can go to when they do not understand what is going on in their head, and that will help them work through stuff. This will help you to avoid one of the biggest problems that could bite you later as your child gets older. When you keep putting your child in time out when they do something wrong, then they will start to withdraw themselves whenever they are emotional, especially through their teenage years.

If, instead, you teach them to talk to you instead, this will also spill into their teenage years and help you to keep your relationship with them strong.

Repairing Relationships After Conflict

I know that no matter how much you try to do everything right, you will be caught off guard sometimes and say the wrong things or fail to communicate with your child like you should. You could just be having a bad day at work and then express that toward your kid without even noticing. So many parents do this. Because your relationship with other people can make you mad, mad, angry, among other things, you might get worked up but suppress those emotions just to get through the day. However, those emotions can linger at the back of your mind, and then you lash out at your child, who does not have anything to do with why you are mad.

This can also happen from your child's side; you can fail to read your child's emotions when they come back from school and then interpret them as an attitude toward you when they are just going through something. These things make conflict blow up between the two of you, even over seemingly small things. As the parent, you need to be the gatekeeper and make sure these emotions do not come into your interactions with your child in the first place.

But let us be honest, this is easier said than done. Sometimes, you will lose it and get emotional even though you know you are not supposed to, and you need to know how to resolve these flare-ups before they negatively affect your relationship with your child. The first thing you need to do is give yourself and your child space to breathe. Go away and allow your child some space to think and breathe while you do the same. Communicate this clearly with your child before you walk away. You can say, "Hey, I noticed you are not happy, and I am sorry. I will give you some time to think, and I will do the same, so maybe we can have this conversation later."

After you have had time to think, it is now time to go back and resolve the issue. I want you to apologize first, all the time. Do not apologize for anything you did not do. That is not a good lesson to teach your child. Be honest and genuine in your apology, and then follow it up with an explanation of what happened, and invite your child to respond. If you do this with them enough, your child will end up understanding and mirroring how you communicate. So, they will also start with an apology and then continue to explain what happened.

Following the make-up session, have a big hug and then look back at what you still need to do to fix the situation that got you there in the first place. If it is something that your child has done wrong, you still need to address it and make it right. If it is a pending task, it still needs to be done and ticked off.

Overall, disciplining your child is never easy. It might seem like there are too many things to consider and too many questions to answer before you can do it, but not really. The only important thing is to ask yourself if you are doing this to develop your child or for your benefit. That's it; if you are disciplining your child because you love them and want them to prosper, then you will make sure the discipline is not damaging to them and their future, and you will make sure that it helps them become a better person.

You are a great parent; I know this because otherwise, you would not be here reading this part of the book. The weakness of good parents, unfortunately, is that they can overthink how they should raise their children or create the connection so much that they end up making the wrong decision. Do not beat yourself up. You are doing well, and you are going to help your child become the person you envision. We are now going to move on and talk about intentional listening so you can improve your communication skills with your child like never before.

Chapter 6: Intentional Listening

One time, I was at a fair with a couple of friends, walking around and having the time of our lives. The place was packed with people and activity, we could hardly hear each other. Amid all that action and noise, we were having a conversation about when we would next meet and how one of my friends was moving to another city since their partner had gotten a promotion at work.

I bet no one else heard what we were talking about, and we sure had no idea what the shouting masses around us were going on about. We could hear a lot of stuff, but we only listened to what each other was saying, and everything else became part of the background. We filtered out all the noise and were still able to have a conversation because we were intentional about listening to each other. Then, suddenly, there was a loud bang a few feet away. One of the stands selling corn dogs had a gas explosion, and the whole table had gone up in flames. This scared us, and we all stopped our conversation to look at what was happening.

After people had put out the fire, and we were safely driving away, I remember one of my friends making a remark about how no matter how loud it gets, if you think you are in trouble, that sound will go above everything else. It is like an alarm that begs for your attention. As he said this, I thought to myself, *we must really value conversation with each other as well because we were also able to hear each other despite all the noise around.*

It seems there is a lesson to be learned there: if you listen intently, then your mind will prioritize that sound over all others. It is almost as if we have selective listening and will hear everything but only choose to listen to what we want to listen to. That is also true when it comes to your relationship with your child. You need to learn to do more than just hear them; you also need to listen to them despite the noise that is around.

Sometimes, the noise that is around is not even literal audible noise, but it can be all the other things that are grabbing your attention as well. In this chapter, we will go over how you can keep your focus and your mind on your child and learn to listen intentionally for better and more effective communication.

Mindful Presence in Conversation

The first step to listening well is to learn to be present when your child is talking to you. Imagine you are in a room having a conversation with someone, and while you are in the middle of talking, they get up and walk out of the room without saying anything. You are left trying to raise your voice so they can still hear you wherever they are or wondering if you should stop and continue when they come back.

When it happens, you will feel like they do not care about what you are saying and that you do not matter enough to get the attention you need. With kids, you do not even have to walk out of the room; if you so much as move away from them even slightly to the side, they will feel like you are not listening to them, and you do not care what they say. One thing I noticed was that when I was working on something and having casual conversations with my child, they would follow my every step even though we were in the same room. If I moved to another point, they would be right next to me, and when I moved back, they did so with me.

Kids see physical distance as a barrier to communication, even in times when it is not. So, if you are going to show that you care about what they are saying, then you will need to be physically present, as close as you can to them. One trick to do this is to try and have your hand on the side of their arms or even over their shoulders as you talk. By having your hands on your child's arms, you ascertain that you are close enough that they feel safe and attended to.

Having your hands on your child's arms will also help to create a safe space between the two of you. It feels like you have just built walls around the two of you that no one else can get through, and you are there to listen to them and only them. If you are standing, you will notice that you will have to scoot down to have your arms on your child's shoulders or on the side of their arms, bringing you closer to them still. You can also have your hands on your child's cheeks if you want, as this is just the same but more intimate and works best when your child is comfortable with it already.

Overall, the point is to make sure you put a lot of effort into getting close to your child when you want to have a conversation with them. This is not something that you need to do every time you want to have a chat with your child. However, this can certainly help to make those moments of communication feel closer and prioritized. This can be the demarcation between casual conversations with your child and the serious ones where you must pay a lot of attention. Either way, you need to prioritize how physically close you are to your child when you are listening to them talk.

The Power of Silence: Inviting Children to Share Without Pressure

After you have gotten your child to feel that you are there, it is time to get them to say what they really want to say. The major thing you need to understand is that humans have layers. In some cases, we do not even know ourselves the way that we hope we do. It is not easy to understand our emotions, and we can very easily fail to articulate what we are really feeling. However, if given enough time to vent or talk about what is bothering you, one thing that will eventually happen is that you will start to get more and more accurate.

In the end, you will address what the real issue is and realize that what you started off with had nothing to do with the real issue or was just a trigger for the emotions. This will be the same with your child. You are supposed to give them time to talk so that they figure out their emotions. Your child will even have deeper layers because their mind has not yet fully formed, and they do not have a good cognition system.

Think about it this way: When a child is playing with another child, and there is this one special toy that they both want, it is not that they both want to play with the toy. Often, the issue is that they do not want the other child to play with the toy while they can't. That is why you can give them the toy, and a moment later, they will leave it and even go for the other toy that their friend is playing with. The point is that the action is supported by the idea that they want to play with the toy, but that is not correct. They have other intentions driving them to want to play with the toy.

Your job as a parent is to help your child figure out why they do the things they do and how you can help them stop doing these things. The child needs to figure out their error themself and not be told. If you give them a chance to say it out loud by arranging their own thoughts in speech, then that will be far more effective than anything else that we can do.

How it plays out practically is you just stay quiet and keep listening to your child even when they think they are done talking. It is such a powerful maneuver; it can even help when you are having a conversation with other adults. You will give them a chance to keep their mind active and look for a deeper truth than the one they just told you. The trick is to stay at the same level of focus and even ask them to say more if they seem hesitant. People love being listened to when they talk, but they often think that the other person does not really have time to listen to everything they have to say, so they speed through a shallow version of their opinion.

You can use this to show extra care and attention: Instead of walking away from the conversation, you can keep at it and show that you are interested in what they have to say and that they do not have to dial down what they really need to let out. Your child will start to talk again if you just give them the space, time, and encouragement to keep on going.

You can use nodding to show that you are listening and still involved or occasionally throw in "yes" and "go on," to show them that you want to hear more. The more you do this, the more they will be comfortable giving you the full story from the start. Active and intentional listening is not always about you, it is about making the other person feel comfortable enough to say what is on their mind.

Reflective Listening

Now that you know how to give the person attention and allow them to talk, it is time to learn how to do reflective listening. This is a process of listening that sets you up as a mirror that reflects what the other person is saying. Your child needs to see your emotions and how you are reacting to what they are saying. If you have mastered the first two points we went over, then you will not have a hard time doing this. You are already physically present, so it will be very easy for your child to see your emotions and reactions on your face.

As you listen and allow your child to talk about how they feel, take some time to think about how you feel listening to them. You could feel excited, happy, sad, or angry, anything really. Now, I want you to allow your face to loosen up and naturally reflect the emotions you are feeling. This acts as even more confirmation that you are listening to them. Remember how we talked about children reading emotions more than words sometimes? This is where some of that comes in handy.

I want you to pretend your face is a mirror, and your child will be able to see the reflection of what they are saying on it.

This will do two things for the conversation: Firstly, you will be able to get deeper emotions on both ends, and second, you will become part of the story and not someone who is listening. This will improve your connection with your child and help you to have more of these kinds of conversations even in the future.

Now, the idea with reflective listening is not to just show the emotions that your child is showing in their speech and move on. Sometimes, you can show complementary emotions instead. Imagine it like this: If your child is afraid of doing something and they are telling you about it, you should not show that you are afraid they might fail as well, rather, you should show faith and hope. You should reflect a belief that they can do anything they set their mind to if they work hard at it.

So, when you listen to your child, you need to be intentional about the message that you send back to them. You do not want it to confirm their shame, guilt, or fears, but rather encourage your child to move forward. Because you will have followed all the other principles of intentional listening, this will not come off as trying to brush away their feelings, they will understand that you are genuinely feeling how they feel and care about them. Your care will shine right through if you stand by them and show that uninterrupted focus and attention.

Encouraging Open Communication

Now, once you have mastered and know how to show reflective listening, it is time to move on to harnessing the power of open communication. Communication is a very complicated thing, and both you and your child have layers, like we went over earlier. You both need to learn to keep getting more and more connected in communication until you are having candid, open, and honest conversations with ease.

This will not be very hard as you are starting out, but the older your child gets, the more they will become their own person. Their opinions will become better formed, and they will start to have things that they are afraid to tell. You will, therefore, need to learn to grow with your child and grow your levels of trust as you do so (Sofer, 2023). We will have a conversation about trust in a later section of this chapter.

To cultivate open communication, you will need to start teaching your child about vulnerability and how to encourage open communication with your child. Vulnerability is the ability for you and your child to tell each other everything, including and especially the things you are afraid to tell each other. This means you will have to start sharing and showing your child what that looks like so that they can do the same with you.

This should not be too hard since you have already started to do this with emotions. You can easily branch from sharing your emotions to adding stories to show how sometimes you make mistakes and that you admit them, and you move on with the intention of becoming a better person. By sharing how you had a bad day at work and because of that, you did not really do as good of a job as you could have, you are teaching your child to do the same.

Your child is not perfect; they will make mistakes, and they need to know that it is okay to make mistakes and talk about them. They need to know that they can come to you with their mistakes, and instead of judging them, you will help them figure out ways to become better next time. After you start sharing with your child, they will feel more comfortable being as open with you as you are with them, and that is where the cycle of having open conversations will start. Once this gets started, you can continue and build confidence and trust between you and your child, as this is the glue that is going to keep you and your child close through time.

Cultivating Trust

Trust is not something you just automatically have as a parent; you must work hard for it. You have to put in time and effort to plant and water the seeds of trust if you want your child to end up trusting you with any and every conversation. I talk to so many parents who have kids who are now grown, and they often complain about how they feel like they are not connected to their children. They feel like there is a lack of trust between the two of them, and these kids are willing to tell the whole world something before they tell their own parents.

This is what you are trying to avoid. You need to build trust now so that when you need it, you will have it already. If your child cannot trust you with their life now, they never will. If you are not their go-to point of confidence, you will have a really hard time becoming that latter. So, let us look at how you can create that now so that you will not have to work harder than you need to later.

Be Honest and Transparent With Your Child

Never lie to your child. I know as a parent, you might feel like the lie will protect or make your child feel better, but trust me, it will only ruin the trust that should be between you and your child. Think about it from your point of view: If you find out your friend, or boss, has been lying to you or keeping information from you, how would you feel? Regardless of the reason, how will it make you feel? You will have a hard time trusting them after that, and so will your child if they find out you are lying to them. You need to make sure you are always honest and completely transparent with your child. I always say, "transparenting," is the best type of parenting. Be a transparent parent, and your child will trust you. Otherwise, they will think you are always hiding something behind your back.

Be Consistent in Your Words and Actions

This one is even harder to do, but you need to be consistent in what you say and what you do. Your child will take what you do over what you say at any time. They are going to always prioritize your actions over everything else, and when they feel like your words are not reflective of what you do, they will feel like you are lying. This will bring you back to the initial problem with lying, and you will lose the trust you are trying so hard to build.

You should try your best to make sure that you live your words, but if you fail, it is okay, you still need to handle that transparently. Have a conversation with your child, tell them you realize you failed to do what you said you would, and that is not good. Tell them you would have loved to do it, but you failed, and you will try again. This will help you to salvage the situation and keep the trust, as the child will see that you still stand by your word even when you do not live up to it.

Be Respectful of Your Child's Feelings and Opinions

Yes, you are older, you know better, you are smarter, and all those other things, but your child is still very important. Juvenile as they can be, your child's opinions mean a lot to them, and they want to feel like those opinions are valued and mean something to you. They will start off by sharing parts of their opinions and wait to see how you will react to them. When they see that you are respectful of their opinion, your child will go ahead and share more as they trust that you will listen and not judge them.

On the other hand, however, if you do not respect the opinions and views of your child, they will simply feel like you do not care about them and withdraw from telling you anything. Another mistake you can make is listening and trying to always have a solution for your child, which will also have a negative impact on them.

Be Patient and Understanding

Patience is the ability to wait for your child to get comfortable instead of forcing them to open up when they are not ready to do so. You need to be able to give your child space and time to get comfortable and slowly open up to you. You can do a lot of things, but you can never force a connection. You need to give it the time it needs to naturally develop. Understand your child and give them time to grow and understand themselves better.

Be Supportive and Encouraging

When you have given your child the space to express themselves, and they have done so, then it is time for you to support and encourage them. It is great that you will be able to hear what your child has to say and that they can trust you with all that information, but it is a complete loss if you cannot convert that into opportunities to help your child. I am not saying you should listen with the intention of providing a solution every time your child comes to you. However, it would be great if you were able to give them advice that would help build them and help them grow the path that you want them to. Part of trusting you with their problems is your child saying they also trust your advice and feedback, so whenever you have something that might be able to assist them, do not hesitate to share it with your child.

Be Willing to Forgive Your Child When They Make Mistakes

Show mercy and grace to your child, or else they will not entrust you with their mistakes. You do the same as an adult as well. Are you comfortable telling people about your mistakes, knowing they will hold them against you and harshly judge you because of it? Certainly not, and so you should not do the same with your child. I do not mean you should not discipline your child when they tell you that they have done something right. If you remember what we said about discipline earlier, you will know that it is the most merciful and gracious approach to take.

Your child should know that when they come to you, they are going to be safe and not have to worry about how they will fix the mistake. You will lead them to that resolution with patience and understanding so they can calmly tell you about their problems and know that you will be there and lead them to the solution that prepares them for the future.

Be a Role Model for Your Child

I could never emphasize this point enough times: You must be the leader and show your child all of the things you want them to eventually become. You will have to become the role model that they can copy and imitate, and that is how you influence your child. While they listen to your words, your child is mostly going to react to the things you do instead. You are a leader in this situation, and there is not much you can do about it. Do not let the opportunity to be a better person pass you, see the challenge to be your child's role model as a challenge to become a better person, in general, and this might be the push you need to become more of who you are born to be.

Empathetic Responses: Connecting on a Deeper Emotional Level

Last but certainly not least, the more empathetic you are toward your child, the deeper the connection you will create with them, and the more you will be able to get candid with them. Empathetic responses are what will make your child come back to you next time, no matter what. If they know that you are waiting for them with open arms and the first thing you will try to do is understand them, then they will always run to you whenever they need your assistance.

Empathy allows you to become your child's emotional buddy, the person who understands their emotions. Once that happens, you have broken down all the walls, and you can expect your child to be free with you and trust you with your words and life. Trust is very important; it is key to the development of a parent-child relationship, so much so that if you are not careful, you will have stunted growth in your relationship simply because you have not unlocked the trust aspect. Trust your child and teach them to trust you.

If there is anything that I learned as I was applying this chapter in my own life, it is that listening is harder than talking. There is so much that goes into it, and sometimes, we do not even really think about it or notice it. Maybe it is because we do not even know what intentional listening is, and that is why it seems easy despite how hard it is.

Now that you know how to listen intentionally, I challenge you to use this trick with all your relationships. This will not only help you with your relationship with your child, but it will help you with your relationships with family, colleagues, and friends as well. Most of what we have gone over in this book is like that, it is not just applicable to you and your child, but to all your other relationships as well. I know you will see an increase in connection between you and your child as you continue to listen to them actively and show up in their life when you need them to.

This is important because it is going to help you very much as you approach the next chapter, which will focus on instilling the right values into your child. The best way to teach someone something is by showing it, but the best way to reiterate it is through communication. I know your newly sharpened communication skills will really help you instill values of respect, compassion, and responsibility into your child as you prepare them to enter the world.

Chapter 7: Instilling Values of Compassion and Responsibility

Creating a relationship with your child is fun. You get a chance to experience the world through a fresh set of eyes. There is nothing more precious than how your relationship with your child will remind you of all the wonder in the world that we forget about as we get more and more entangled with the business of each day. That is the gift you get from your children, the joy of experiencing life with them and sharing the wonder that still exists in their eyes.

In return, you get the chance to prepare your child for the future and introduce them to the values that will guide them for the rest of their life. If you do not do this, they will have their morals and principles shaped by everyone else around them, and you cannot trust anyone else to do that. You have the responsibility, or should I call it the honor, of teaching your child all the principles they will need to find their footing and grow in the world. Among all the principles you will teach to your child, the two most important will be compassion and responsibility.

Your child will be a force for good if they practice compassion and responsibility. Compassion is your child's ability to set out to always do good in the world. On the other hand, responsibility is the ability of your child to stand and act where it is needed and to accept accountability for their actions. If you have someone who accepts accountability for their actions and whose heart and mind are completely set on doing right, then you can use that person to lead their community and bring the best out of it. You have the chance to raise such an individual in your child.

Since we have already gone over how to build a relationship with your child, the rest will be easy. You only need to keep with the principles we went over in the first few chapters, and the rest will fall into place. If you communicate with your child in love and respect and allow them to grow in the protection of your presence, all that is left is to intentionally point them toward compassion and responsibility, show them a few examples, and you will be set to go.

Mindful Teaching of Values

The mistake that most parents make is that they think their child will grow up with good values naturally. This is especially true for parents who keep their children protected from the world and, therefore, assume that since the child does not get to witness the evil ways of the world, they will grow into responsible and upstanding citizens. Unfortunately, it does not work this way, goodness is not a default setting in children. While they will start out naive and somewhat oblivious to the evil of the world, that does not equate to being good.

If you are not intentional about teaching your child good morals and values, then they will easily become everything you are trying to protect them from becoming. I know it is not easy to teach your children all the values that you want them to have, but I will walk you through some ways through which you can do this in a way that really shapes your child into the person you want them to be.

The key is to build on good foundations, if you teach your child the important principles then you will not have to worry about most of the other stuff. I truly believe that the basis for all good principles is compassion and responsibility. There is something fundamental about these two that will help your child to understand everything else as soon as they understand those two. We will go into how you can build a strong understanding of the two values, compassion and responsibility, and then how you can add everything else on top of that easily.

Teaching Compassion

Compassion is the ability your child has to relate to the feelings of others and respond with care. It is like a language.

Your child will have to learn how to hear first, understand what the other person is feeling, and then speak back, responding to what they feel the other person is communicating. This gives us the two pillars of compassion: empathy and kindness.

"Empathy is being able to know how someone else is feeling, even when you aren't in the same situation" (Bryant, 2022, para. 1). Empathy and kindness can be hard concepts to understand and learn how to do both.

Empathy

The best way to teach your child to be empathetic is to show empathy to them yourself. Remember, your child is going to be mostly a product of what you do with them, but by showing them that you can understand how they feel in different situations, like we went over earlier, you create a connection in their brain that tells them that understanding others is something they can do.

Your child does not really have an idea that something exists until they see it happening, and that is where you come in. With empathy, you need to show them examples of this in your own relationship with them and, from there, teach them to do the same. One easy way to do this is through communicating emotions. When your child is going through something, and they throw a tantrum or they are just off, and you notice, go and strike up a chat about feelings.

Start with something like, "I think you are feeling sad. Is that true?" From there, let them explain to you how they feel until you understand and can really relate to what they tell you. Then and only then, can you try to find a solution with them about what they are feeling. Make sure you show that it is important for you to understand how they feel. Ask questions about how they feel and keep going over it until they really understand why you are so concerned.

Now, the next time you are having an interaction with them, give them a chance to understand your feelings in return. You can start this conversion with something like, "I *think* I am angry." By saying you *think*, instead of saying that you *are* a certain way, you give them a chance to run a diagnosis on whether you really are angry. After you say this, allow your child to ask you questions about why you might feel that way and try to figure out how to help you.

You can even lead them into the conversion if they do not seem to understand the prompt. You can say something like, "Can you help me to figure out why I feel like this, or if I ever really feel like this." If you try this enough, your child will learn to do it by themselves. When you are not looking happy, they will come and ask you what is wrong and genuinely try to figure out what is bothering you. That is what you are aiming for: A situation where your child can see when someone is not okay and genuinely cares.

If your child is asking you how you are, they are concerned about all the other kids and people they meet as well, and this is how you get them to start showing empathy to the world around them. Now remember, empathy is only half of compassion, so you will need to help your child show kindness in action to the people who need it.

Kindness

I remember a cousin who went to mechanic school but then dropped out to pursue his passion for painting. He has done very well in his art career, far better than those who stayed in mechanics, but he was a brilliant student. My father and I cannot help but make fun of him every now and then because he can always tell what is wrong with the car, but he cannot fix it. Because he never finished school, he never quite learned how to get dirty and tear the car apart, fixing the problems, but he knows what is wrong with it from revving it a few times and checking the engine.

I like to think of teaching a child kindness is like teaching them how to fix the car. It is one thing to know something is wrong, but knowing how to fix it is a whole different thing. Imagine it: what good is it for your child to be able to tell when others are not okay but fail to help them after that? Not a lot of good as you can imagine. In fact, this will only make your child feel powerless and like they cannot do any good. But not under your parenting! You will create a child who also knows how to show kindness to the world and bring solutions to problems.

Just like in the previous section, you will help your child by being an example of how to show kindness. Think of it as a journey: You are the guide, and you are showing your child where to step. You will have to start by showing your child the kindness that you want them to show to the world.

It is easy to show your child kindness, you get a lot of opportunities to do this throughout the day. However, there is a little flair we are going to add this time that can help make your child understand what you are doing when you show kindness so that they can also reciprocate. I want you to say it to them as you do it, weird as it may sound.

Now, I know you would never do this with an adult. You cannot walk to someone and say, "Hi, I am here to show you kindness by doing this nice thing for you;" it would feel contrived and fake, ruining the intentions you have as you do it. With a child, however, it works differently. Children, yours included, take things at face value. So, when you say something, they take your words as they are and do not think beyond that.

So, the next time your child tells you how they feel, or you are helping them go through something, ask them how you can show them kindness. Explain what kindness is in a way that they will understand. It does not even have to be something complex; you can refer to kindness as anything someone does to make another person feel better or good about themselves. After this, you can ask, "How can I show kindness today?"

Following this up, ask your child to show you some kindness every now and then. Do not do this too much, lest you lose the meaning of it along the way and turn it into the equivalent of asking your child to help around the house. You do not want to ever mix chores and responsibilities with what kindness is. You want them to understand that kindness is when you or they do something nice that they did not really have to do but still choose to do.

When your child starts showing you kindness, it is time to move on to the next step and have them show someone else kindness. The best part about this step is, as soon as they start showing you kindness, then they will start showing it to the people around them as well. Try asking your child if they have been able to show kindness to anyone through the day when you see them at the end of the day. By doing this you are showing them that it is okay to show kindness to others, and they will certainly be more aware and look out for chances to do it when they go out for the day.

You can then start having more elaborate conversations about kindness because your child will already understand it from your actions and leadership.

So, now that you have gotten them showing compassion, you can walk with your child through conversations around it and talk to them about how they can do even more.

As part of your talks with your child, you can also tell them about some ways they can be compassionate and show kindness to the people around them. Below are some ideas to get you started with the conversation. Feel free, however, to add anything that comes to mind or that is specific to your child.

- Hold the door open for someone.
- Say "please" and "thank you."
- Share their toys.
- Help around the house.
- Be a good friend.
- Be kind to animals.
- Be kind to the environment.

Larry Roy Olson

Environmental Awareness

As much as your child must be kind and compassionate to the people they interact with, they also need to be compassionate to the environment they exist in. This is a very crucial element, now more than ever, because of the state that our world is in. The unfortunate part is that there is very little our generation can do about the problem, we are, after all, a big part of the problem.

It will take three generations to bring our beautiful blue planet back to good health. The first can be us, teaching the next generation about preserving and caring for the environment from a young age so that they grow up conscious of this problem. The next generation will see a decline in pollution and then, finally, curb the continued wasteful habits that have been choking the planet. The third and final generation will be our grandchildren, who, on top of not littering, will start to reverse what we did and find ways of cleaning up the world we will leave for them.

If this is going to happen in the coming generations, then you must play your part and teach your child about our world and how we take care of it. You can even take your child into nature to see the beauty that it holds and teach them to find peace in the embrace of nature. This will help them to learn the importance of the ecosystem they exist in and their part in making sure it survives.

Teach your children to love and care for animals as well. They, too, have a part to play in how our world is. We have a responsibility to look after all life and everything that nature has gifted us with. Add lessons of gratitude along with the lessons on how to take care of the Earth. We should be grateful for all the food, the air, and countless resources that we get from the Earth. Our responsibility is to at least make sure we will still be able to get those resources in the coming centuries by taking good care of what we have.

Teaching Kids to Appreciate Life's Blessings

It is not just nature that your child needs to be grateful for, but all the gifts that life brings our way. Gratitude is a great way to maintain a healthy mind, and the earlier you learn it, the more effective it will be for you. When you are grateful, your mind is in a state of abundance, looking at all that you have instead of living in a state of greed, looking at everything you do not have and desiring it regardless of the cost.

Again, your child will only do what they see you doing. So, you need to lead your child into a state of gratitude and help them to develop that mindset all on their own. There are several ways to reach your child's gratitude, but I will only share with you, my favorite. I love how this method teaches children to appreciate everything around them, even the really small things and the things you might oversee.

Now, to do this exercise, I want you to see it as a game that you are playing with your child. The aim of the game is to teach your child to recognize what they should be grateful for. So, you will have to come up with a category and write down the list of all the things in that category to be grateful for.

This list can include stuff like the following:

- your health
- your family and friends
- a roof over your head
- food on your table
- clean water to drink
- the ability to read and write
- the freedom to live your life as you choose
- the beauty of nature
- the kindness of strangers
- the opportunity to learn and grow
- the chance to make a difference in the world

Note that you can add anything that comes to mind, especially if it is something in your child's ecosystem and lifestyle. You should also add some events from your life that are specific and that your child can relate to. Maybe you bought a new car, you got a new job, or it is just a family member that you want your child to be grateful for.

I want you to then ask to go over these with your child so that they have a good understanding of what they must be grateful for. Go over the list with your child and ask them what sticks out to them the most.

You can do this through questions as follows:

- Are you grateful for the clean water you have for drinking?
- Are you grateful for the way the birds sing in the morning?
- Are you grateful for the chance to go to school and learn?

After each question, you can then explain to your child what it means to be grateful for some of these things. For example, your child probably has no idea that there are so many people on Earth who do not have access to clean drinking water. You can then explain that to your child so that they understand why it is a blessing that they have clean water for drinking and cooking.

This exercise is meant to show your child that they are important and that they have been blessed with things that other people have. This will help them to see why they have to show gratitude and steward what they have well. The main point is to teach them to have a positive attitude toward life and nurture a grateful heart that will be content with what it has.

This also goes back to what we said about compassion: The more your child understands how fortunate they are, the more they will use their resources to help others who are less fortunate. When people are not grateful, they become greedy, and instead of giving when they can, they will try to take as much as they can. You cannot afford to raise a self-absorbed child whose only concern is themself and what they can get. Doing this will make parenting hell for you, but more than that, it will make life very hard for the child as well.

Fostering Social Responsibility

Humans depend on each other for the expansion of civilization and the strengthening of the moral code. We are a dependent species such that no one can make it alone. Think about it: We have been able to delegate different things to different people so that we can become very effective and efficient with everything that we do. For example, some people work in food production so that you do not have to, while others are focused on providing entertainment, and yet others do a lot of other different things.

Look around you, you have no idea how much of the world around you works. From how your phone works, how the food in your fridge is produced, how the furniture you are using is made, all the way to how this book was printed or recorded. You do not have to understand; you live in a community where everyone does their part so that no one person has to do everything. You also have your part to play, small or big. Your work contributes at some level to a service or product that benefits a lot of other people who would have no idea how to do it if it was not for you.

You need to make sure that your child understands that they are an asset to the society they live in. They have an obligation to bring the best of themselves and apply their efforts as much as they can. Everyone has something to offer to the world at every stage of their life. Teach your child to be respectful to elders and greet them when they see them on the street. Teach them to help others when they can, to stand up when they see bullying at school, and to speak up for what they know is right.

If your child does not see themselves as a part of society—a valuable part of society—then they will fail to develop most of the virtues and values we have gone over (*Role of society*,

2021). For instance, why would they need to be accountable to a society they do not care about? Why would they ever become responsible or compassionate, unless they see the connection they have to the community and realize their actions contribute to the whole society?

The best way to do this, as always, is to show your child how you are giving back to society. You do not have to be running a soup kitchen or have big events for the community to share how you contribute, you can talk about the small and simple things. Being a good citizen comes down to the small details anyway, the way you are considerate and polite with others, returning the shopping cart after you take the groceries out, separating your trash so it is recyclable, offering help when you can to the people who need it and everything else you can do.

Standing Up Against Bullying: Building Courage and Moral Integrity

I have heard so many people teach about standing up for oneself in a way that gives the wrong results altogether. You need to teach your child to stand up for themselves, but you need to do it right lest you create the bully you are trying to protect your child from. Most people will say to their kids, "Do not let anyone say anything to you that you do not like," or "Do not let people look down on you." If that happens, then you need to stand up for yourself and fight for yourself. You should not just stand there and watch if other kids are going to hurt you.

The problem with this is, it is the exact mentality that most bullies have. They have this belief that they should always be at the top and will not let anyone be better than them. Driven by this, they will start hitting others and showing aggression because they feel threatened by the other kids and fear they might lose relevance unless they do something to assert dominance.

Instead, I want you to teach your child that they are enough and that they do not need to prove anything to anyone. Your child must have faith in themself and be able to show that confidently when they go out. Teach them how to show others compassion and help if they see anyone being treated unfairly. By doing this, you give your child the confidence that gives them a voice whenever they see something wrong.

First, your child must learn to defend what is right before you tell them to defend themselves. They should not just hate bullying because they do not want to be hurt or bullied, but because they understand that it is wrong and no one deserves to go through it. When you do this, your child will become the point of hope for all the other kids around them, and they will help other kids to speak and stand up for themselves if anything happens. The only thing that can be more powerful than bullying is the ability to stand your ground and confidently talk against it, even in the face of the bully.

Once your child has learned this, they will feel free to tell you about it if it happens, along with the teachers and anyone else who can help. The most dangerous thing, and the reason bullying can be so prevalent in some kids' circles, is because the kids are too afraid to even talk about it, and so the teachers and parents do not really know it is happening. But if one kid out of the whole bunch is vocal about it and stands strong on those convictions, then the leaders will get involved sooner and be able to help the whole bunch.

The Ripple Effect: How Small Acts of Kindness Create Positive Change

You need to understand that while all the actions we talked about in this book and the suggestions I give are small, they will have a far greater impact in the end. Think of the butterfly effect. If a butterfly flaps its wings, no matter how tiny they are, given the right circumstances and time, that small flap can move and grow to become a current that will sweep the ocean onto the land in tsunamis. It is a small action that will have a great impact in the future. This is also the phenomenon with ripples in water, hence the name. If you throw a stone into the water, the ripple will start out very small, but as they go out, they become bigger and bigger.

This is what the actions you are teaching your child will do as well. Think of it this way: You cannot really teach your child to open and run a soup kitchen at the age of 5, but you can teach them to share what they have with others. The fun part is that it takes the same heart to be able to share at 5 as it does to become a person who can change the world at 30. So, while you might feel like you are doing very little by teaching your child all these small ideas and acts of kindness, I want you to know that you are planting a seed. Just like the sequoia tree, which grows into a monster from a very small seed, your child will become great and impactful from the small actions that you are teaching them now.

Never despise where you start off from. It is okay if you are having a hard time even teaching the simple things like thank you and please. You will eventually get there. Remember, your child is like a sponge, they absorb what they see around them. They absorb what they see in your life and the energy that you let out. On that point, if you do your best to raise them right and give them the chance to develop themselves, even if you fail to see it happen now, that seed will have been planted.

So, do not give up hope; do not ever think maybe this is not for you. Having the heart and ambition to see your child's life change is really all you need. If you have the drive and the information, then you will always make something great work out. That is what I am inviting you to believe and hold on to. Your positivity and will to see your child succeed well have an impact on them, and that is nearly inevitable.

The small acts of goodness you show them and teach them will create core memories in their minds that will remain a part of their mental frame of reference even as adults. This is the time when your child is easiest to influence, and you should really do so and do so with all you have. As your child builds these schemas that they will use to see the world, I want you to be there, throwing in your suggestions for how they ought to orient themselves.

Thank you for all the work you have done making sure your child will become a good force in the community. This is perhaps the most selfless part of this entire book. Training your child to have these morals and values will benefit the community and society they will live in more than it does yourself and the child. You are teaching them to care for others, even at their own expense, and that is a true act of bravery. You are making a hero out of your child.

I want you to keep drilling these principles into them as they grow. You are the line between creating the hero and the villain. Your child is in an open book with blank lines, and you have the first chance to write in it. You can influence what they do before the rest of the world does, and if you miss out on that chance, your child will become what the world is. Your child mirrors what they see, and you do not want them to mirror all the negativity that is in the world, rather, you want them to become conduits of positivity as they mirror all the lessons you have taught them.

Now that you have built such a strong basis for values, rooted in responsibility and compassion, let us look at how your parenting journey can remain sustained and consistent as your child grows older. This is not a one-time job; you cannot just teach your child these values or build this relationship in a few days and think that that will be enough to carry you through the years. It does not work like that; you will have to be willing to put in a lot of effort and make sure that the efforts are maintained in the long run.

Chapter 8: Your Mindful Parenting Journey

I want you to do something important, something you should do at least four to five times every week as you continue on your parenting journey. I want your journal. If you do already, then that is great, and if not, it is time to get started. I want you to get a journal where you will write about and discuss with yourself how the parenting journey is going.

This is about you: It is your journey. Yours and your child's. You cannot just read this book and think that is enough; you have an obligation to take this book and personalize it. In a way, you need to recreate this book in the context of your relationship with your child and how they are growing with you. You can never find two parent-child relationships that are the same. People are so different, and you cannot use the same pill to cure all illnesses. However, you can use a template and customize it to fit the uniqueness of your relationship with your child.

If you have not found a way to personalize this information and make it even more relevant to your relationship with your child, that is okay. You do not have to read or listen to this book once. You can have another go at it, and make sure you are applying all that you are learning as you do so. The more you apply, the more you learn, the more you internalize. You can do it. If you have gotten to this point, I believe you can do anything. You are good enough and powerful enough to create the life you want for your children.

Now, let us look at how you can use the journal to record and improve your journey as a parent. Once you get here, you are at the beginning of that journey. I know you might have thought that would have happened at the start of the book, but no. You have so much to do, and the first seven chapters were more like training in order for you to become the parent you need and want to be. They were there to show you how you can create a relationship with your child, communicate with them, and show them love. Now, you get to start the long journey of doing all of these things.

To get you started, let's talk about you. Let's talk about what you need to do apart from your child to effectively apply all that we have talked about in your life and relationship with your child.

First! Love Yourself

Like I said before, you can never pour from an empty tank, you cannot love your child if you do not love yourself. You cannot give your child the attention and care that you want if you have never given it to yourself. Everything you do, especially parenting, comes from your mind. All you are doing is looking at ideas in your mind and using them to frame how you interact and lead your child. If you do not have a handle on concepts like responsibility and compassion, how will you be able to share them with your child? It will be close to impossible.

So, the challenge is to learn to love yourself first before you go ahead and try to love your child. If you have been having a hard time loving yourself, do not worry, according to Cooks-Campbell (2022), self-love is a skill you can develop—much like self-confidence or self-trust. It is not too late to learn how to love yourself so you can love your child. If your child can see how much you care for yourself, they will learn to do the same for themselves and give you the respect that you give yourself. Self-love is the beginning of all the other forms of love; prioritize yourself so that you will have enough love and energy to extend that care to your child.

There are three specific things that I do to continuously show myself love and make sure that despite the world trying to bring me down, I always rise in the end. The three practices are self-care, self-acceptance, and balancing my work and family in a healthy way. I have been doing this for so long now that these three things have merged and become such a part of my lifestyle that I do not even have to think about doing them, they are a part of me.

Practicing Self-Care

You are human, and that means you need to take extremely good care of yourself. Humans are very strong and resilient, but if you blink for a moment and stop taking care of yourself, you can deteriorate faster than you can imagine. You need to be intentional about taking care of your body and mind all the time. The best way to do this is by building habits that promote healthy living so that you do not have to always think about what you should do to care for yourself.

The best part is that most of these things are very easy to integrate into your life, and so they become a seamless extension of your existence. The three main things you should add to your life to maintain your health are good sleep, good nutrition, and exercise. I know there are so many other things you can do to keep yourself in top shape, but if you have these tied down, then it will make a good basis for you to do everything else.

The reason sleep, nutrition, and exercise are important is that with only one of them off, your whole life will start to deteriorate. If you do not get enough sleep, your body will fail to use the nutrition you are taking properly, and that will then affect how effective your exercises will be as well. Failing to keep any of these three will have the same effect on the entire process.

Self-Acceptance

Self-acceptance is all about forgiving yourself and accepting your mistakes and shortfalls. So many people live in self-hate and walk around covered in shame, guilt, and blame for what they have done, or failed to do in life. You should hold yourself accountable for everything you do, but you cannot allow that to make you lose your self-love.

Remember, the love you give to your child is a direct result of the love that you have for yourself. Because of this, you need to make sure that you deal with your failures in a progressive way. The way that I do this is through journaling. Journaling allows you to let go of the things that weigh your mind and get some level of peace.

Balancing Work and Family

You will need to make sure that you appropriately distinguish between your work and family time and then give each the time it needs to thrive. You cannot have either your work or family as an afterthought, both must be given care. Most people see their family as the section of their life that just comes after they finish work and sustains them until they have to go back again in the morning. This inconveniences your family to some extent and makes it hard for you to apply all the ideas we have been talking about.

What you should do is make a schedule and intentionally plan out the activities you want to do with your family. You do not want your child to feel like they are an afterthought, so you combat this by planning out what you are going to do with them and telling them ahead of time. This will create a feeling of anticipation and let them know that you look forward to the time you get to spend with them as well.

Celebrating Progress

I want you to be intentional about celebrating every single success that you reach with your child. Celebrating is like validating success, when you do this, you create a memory that encapsulates the success in your mind for years to come. The photos you take and the fun you have when you celebrate create a reminder in your mind that you can look back on and see how far you have come.

Celebrations are such a great way to bring the people you care about and the people you have been working with into the experience of joy and success that you have. In this case, it will be mostly your family that you will be celebrating with. This will be a moment for you to share the joy of the fruits of all the work you have been putting in with your child or children.

When was the last time you celebrated something? If it has been more than two or three months, then I want you to plan and go for a celebration with your family or children. You can do something simple, like a movie night, have ice cream, or even just go out to eat. The important thing is that you do something to show your gratitude for all that you have been able to achieve through the past few months.

I have a fun experiment that I want you to try at home. With your child or children, I want you to make a jar but paint it so that once inside, no one can tell what is in the jar. You can also use an old shoe box or any other covered container for this as long as it is something that you can close and have little notes slipped into. After setting up the box, explain to the rest of the family that this is a celebration jar. Everyone should add anything that happened to them or another family member that they think should be celebrated and how.

This will get your children to always be aware of all the good happening around them so that they can put something in the jar before the week ends. On one day every week, take out all the notes inside and read them to see what has been submitted. You can then decide what one thing you can go and do with the kids to celebrate all the successes of the week.

On the day, you can then read out the successes so that everyone can cheer and be happy together.

When people hear of celebrating, they think of big events and parties that take time and money to plan and execute. While it would be great if you could have that as part of your celebrations, it does not really matter. You can celebrate however you want to as a family. That could mean getting pizza and sitting together to watch a movie, or it could be a regular dinner with the addition of some dessert and sprinkling confetti around the table. However you want to celebrate is up to you, but you cannot afford to not do it. It is so important that you teach the kids how to celebrate the milestones in their lives (Moran, 2022).

Celebration is not only about being happy, even though that is perfectly healthy and absolutely needed. Celebrations are also about learning to recognize growth and success. If you do not celebrate, your child might fail to notice when something happens, and they ought to be happy. They will end up just going through life uninspired and with no motivation to keep going because they fail to understand what success is and how to measure it.

In addition to this, a celebration is like the closing of a chapter so that we can look at new goals. it is not the attainment of the goal that gives meaning, but the process of pursuing a goal. Because of this, when you have time to recognize the completion of goals, you will also be able to notice when you should create new targets and start working hard to reach them. You will be super motivated to reach the new goal as well since you know there is a celebration and recognition waiting at the end when you achieve it.

Another element that you should use, but sparingly, is the idea of awards and rewards. Rewards can be given throughout the week so that your children understand that good work gets rewarded. When they are still young, children will have a hard time understanding that their good work pays off in the end, even if it is not right away and even if it is not in a way that they can see a correlation. In such cases, it is important to use rewards to create a sense of accomplishment and excitement for them. As they get older, you can then teach them how they can expect to see the results in other forms, and sometimes they will have to wait until later in life.

On the other hand, we have awards, but these cannot be given throughout the week, or even throughout the year. They should be occasional things that you give to your children for really exceptional, outstanding results from what they are doing. This can be in certain behaviors exhibited at home, doing well in school, sports, or anything and everything that gives you a reason to be proud as a parent.

Awards should never be given just so a child feels good. They represent a high level of achievement that is above what your child was expected to achieve. By doing this, you are teaching your children to aim high and do better than they did last time. So, even when they become good at something, they will not stop there but have a thirst for excellence and for doing their very best all the time.

You can do awards once a year and make sure it is a time when you show how the child deserves the award and how others can get it, too, by doing well.

Enjoy the Journey

It can be so easy for you to get carried away in parenting that you forget one of the first principles we started talking about at the beginning of this book. You are your child's friend, and they are your friend. As much as there is a lot of work that will have to be done to get the connection that you desire with your child and a lot to be done to lead your child into being the type of person who will succeed in society, you also need to remember to have fun.

What is a friendship if there is no fun in it? Well, it becomes work, obligations, and everything else that drains the life excitement out of any relationship. This applies to grown-ups as well. You have to create a way to grow your relationships without losing the fun that put them together in the first place. Let's be honest: While there might be some underlying serious reason for friendship, there is always an element of fun that motivates every friendship relationship. You want to be friends with people that you can have fun with, and this goes for your connection with your child as well.

I want you to constantly evaluate your relationship with your child and ask yourself if it is as fun as you want it to be. Do you spend time laughing and having meaningless conversations, or have you turned the relationship into a grind that takes away your joy and peace without you noticing it? When you realize you could use more fun in your relationship, it is time to come up with a plan for how you can do that. If you go back to the start of this book and begin reading again, you will find that there is a laid-back approach to the whole thing that can get lost as you try to figure out how to see the best possible results.

Create your plan to restore fun and see how you can bring the smile back to your child's face again. I want to leave you with some ideas of things that you can do to bring the fun back into your relationship with your child. You can add more if you like or modify these to make sure that they work with what you and your child like and with the lifestyle that you are living.

Play games together as much as you can. These can be board games, video games, or anything else that you can get your hands on. Plug in a game, set a timer for how long you are going to play, and invite your friend.

Go on outings. You can go to the park, the zoo, the museum, or any other place that your child enjoys. This will bring adventure to your relationship, and you will find yourselves relaxed and having fun by the end of the event.

I learned this next one from my mother, who had the habit of reading me a book every night before I went to sleep. I encourage you to read books together with your child every now and then. You can read to them or have them read to you; sometimes, you can even take turns depending on the book and its difficulty level. Reading books together is a great way to bond with your child and help them develop their love of reading.

Watch movies together. Watching movies together is a fun way to spend time with your child and relax. You can even learn their favorite songs from their favorite Disney movies. In addition, this is where you will learn which character is their favorite, which will come in handy if you want to buy them a gift as a good surprise.

Cook together with your child as much as you can. Cooking together is a great way to teach your child about food and how to cook while having loads of fun at the same time.

Take walks together and just talk. Taking walks together is a great way to get exercise and spend time with your child. On these walks, you can talk to your child about nothing and everything just to have fun and banter. Sometimes, the best thing you can do with your child is just talk to them. Talk about their day, their friends, their interests, and anything else that comes up.

The most important thing is to find activities that you and your child enjoy doing together. The more fun you have, the more likely your child is to enjoy spending time with you. Fun is an ingredient that is crucial to your relationship with your child, but admittedly, one that you can easily overlook in the pursuit of the perfect relationship.

Keep your mind alert and evaluate your relationship with your child regularly. As we have gone through, it is important that firstly, you keep an eye on yourself and measure your own mental health and general health as an individual. You do not want to lose yourself in the process. Keep yourself healthy, and make sure you take good care of yourself so that you have the positivity to share with your child. You come first, if you do not take care of yourself, you will not have the energy, will, ability, or the right mindset to care for your child.

It is okay to ask for a time-out for yourself. It is okay to feel tired, and like you need a break. You can take some time away if you have someone else who can look out for the kids for a while. You can see a therapist and get professional help on how you can handle the stress and demands of raising a child. It is not easy, by any means, but I know you can do it and will push through regardless. I urge you to notice how your mental health is and how the relationship is growing through time. You must act as the guard to make sure neither of these things starts to spiral slowly out of your grasp.

Conclusion

Well done! You have made it to the end of this book. This journey to create a strong and effective relationship with your child could not have been, and certainly was not, easy. It is a path that many fail to go on but one that you have gone on and done very well. This is a testament to how much you value your child, your relationship with them, and their future. It is that care and passion to see your child succeed that is important. All this information will not be nearly as effective unless you are moving with the pure intention to see your relationship with your child grow and to see your child make it in life.

Now that you have come to the end, I want you to remain encouraged. You can become a good parent and build connections with your child that will go beyond what you are doing now. You can build with your children a partnership that will carry them into a better future. You have the power to teach your children to become upstanding citizens who are not afraid to stand up and speak for themselves and all those in the community who need a voice. They will be strong and encouraging because of you and bring the best of themselves to the table.

I want you to do something, the last thing you will have to do. I want you to get out your journal again and make one last entry. Thinking back on how your relationship with your child was when you started reading this book, I want you to compare it to how it is now and write down all the highlights. I want you to record all the changes you have noticed between the time you started reading this book and now. Take your time, and remember all the good that you have brought to your child and the rest of your family by just being intentional and applying these basic, fundamental principles.

After you have made a record of all the changes, I want you to feel proud and reward yourself. You might have the feeling that it was this book that gave you all this success, and as much as I appreciate the recognition, it was not just because of this book that you made it. It was because of the work you put in and the consistency you maintained.

Now, think about how your life has changed and how you would want someone else to see the same change that you have seen. I want you to be intentional about this—maybe you read this book when your child had grown a bit, but you know someone who could start using it now. Think of one person who could really use the help in this book, and I want you to give them this copy.

Better yet, you can even buy them a new copy and bless them with it. Another way you can help other people see the results from what you have read is by leaving a review of how you have been impacted by the book. Leave some advice for future readers on how they can prepare for the fun yet transforming journey that this book will take them on. It is the experience that you have had that could help someone else find the growth and connection with their child that you found.

Thank you for learning along with me. I really appreciate it. Now, it is time to go and practice everything, every day, until it all becomes a habit. Go and live the life you want with your child or children. Use everything you have learned to show your children love and care while building for the future they are going to love. May you build a life that helps to fulfill both your and your children's dreams. Never forget, you have the power to shape the future right now, use it wisely. You are the parent your child needs.

References

Bryant, C. D. (2022). *What is empathy? definition for kids.* Talking Tree Books. https://talkingtreebooks.com/teaching-resources-catalog/definitions/what-is-empathy.html

Clark, E. L. M., Jiao, Y., Sandoval, K., & Biringen, Z. (2021). Neurobiological implications of parents–child emotional availability: a review. *Brain Sciences, 11*(8), 1016. https://doi.org/10.3390/brainsci11081016

Cooks-Campbell, A. (2022, May 26). *What self-love truly means and ways to cultivate it.* Better Up. https://www.betterup.com/blog/self-love

Dweck, C. (2017). *Mindset: changing the way you think to fulfil your potential.* Robinson.

Gallo, A. (2023, March 24). *6 Little things you can do every day to make your child more independent.* Parents. https://www.parents.com/kids/development/little-things-you-can-do-every-day-to-make-your-child-more-independent/

Heid, M. (2019, October 15). *Are time-outs harmful to kids? The latest research says otherwise.* Time. https://time.com/5700473/time-outs-science/#:~:text=Call%20says%20time%2Dins%20are

Kadane, L. (2019, March 15). *Cell phone addiction: 4 ways to discuss it with your kids.* Today's Parents. https://www.todaysparent.com/kids/cell-phone-addiction-4-ways-to-talk-to-your-kids/

Mental Health Foundation. (2022). *Body image in childhood.* Mental Health. https://www.mentalhealth.org.uk/explore-mental-health/articles/body-image-report-executive-summary/body-image-childhood

Moran, L. (2022, May 9). *How to bond with your child and celebrate everyday moments.* Celebree School. https://www.celebree.com/blog/resources/how-to-bond-with-your-child-and-celebrate-everyday-moments/

Peterson, J. B., Doidge, N., & Ethan Van Sciver. (2018). *12 Rules For Life: An Antidote To Chaos* (p. 91). Allen Lane.

Raising Children Network. (2017, June 5). *Praise, encouragement and rewards.* Raising Children Network. https://raisingchildren.net.au/toddlers/connecting-communicating/connecting/praise

Role of society in child development. (2021, July 8). Allison Academy. https://www.allisonacademy.com/parents/child-development/role-of-society-in-child-development/

Shapiro, S., & White, C. (2014). *Mindful discipline*. New Harbinger Publications.

Sofer, O. J. (2023). *Leading difficult conversations with mindful presence, with Oren J Sofer*. Mindfulness Exercises. https://mindfulnessexercises.com/podcast-episodes/leading-difficult-conversations-with-mindful-presence-with-oren-jay-sofer/

Larry Roy Olson

Jotham Sewall

Infant Baptism

and ordinance of the gospel

Jotham Sewall

Infant Baptism
and ordinance of the gospel

ISBN/EAN: 9783337887629

Printed in Europe, USA, Canada, Australia, Japan

Cover: Foto ©Lupo / pixelio.de

More available books at **www.hansebooks.com**

INFANT BAPTISM

AN

ORDINANCE OF THE GOSPEL.

By Rev. JOTHAM SEWALL.

APPROVED BY THE COMMITTEE OF PUBLICATION.

BOSTON:

MASSACHUSETTS SABBATH SCHOOL SOCIETY,

DEPOSITORY No. 13 CORNHILL.

CAMBRIDGE:
Allen and Farnham, Printers.

NOTE. — The following essay is the substance of four sermons prepared and preached to the people of my present charge, and also to a neighboring church. Some of the hearers expressed a wish that they should be given to the public through the press; and I have been disposed to comply with this wish, especially as some points connected with the subject, which tend to illustrate it, are not presented in other treatises of the kind. And should this humble effort be the means of confirming the faith of any of the people of God in an important truth, and of stimulating them to a more faithful discharge of parental duties, the labor involved will be abundantly repaid.

J. SEWALL.

NORTH GRANVILLE, N. Y., March 28, 1859.

CONTENTS.

CHAPTER I.

CHAPTER II.

CHAPTER III.

Objections. — Apostles required belief before baptism. — Those who had been circumcised required to be baptized. — Further arguments. — Christ and his apostles taught and practised just as we should have expected if children were still regarded as in covenant with their parents, and just as we should not have expected on the contrary supposition. — No complaints were made by the converted Jews. — Testimony from history.

CHAPTER IV.

Relation of baptized children to the church. — Utility of Infant Baptism. — It tends to increase the faithfulness of parents; to secure to children the prayers and counsels of the church; and to soothe the grief occasioned by their death.

INFANT BAPTISM.

CHAPTER I.

CHURCH DEFINED. — JEWISH CHURCH FORMED. — LIMITED. — JEWISH AND CHRISTIAN CHURCH THE SAME.

An important feature of the government of God is placed before us in the passage, " The mercy of the Lord is from everlasting to everlasting upon them that fear him, and his righteousness unto children's children; to such as keep his covenant, and to those that remember his commandments to do them." (Psalms 103: 17–18.) On the principle here expressed, an institution was founded, under th^e former dispensation, in which, by a religious rite, children were consecrated to God. And the same principle, under the present, involves the propriety and duty of a similar consecration in a solemn religious ordinance.

In our view, Infant Baptism occupies a place in the system of God's mercy to men, which invests it with unspeakable importance; and the best good of the church and the world, we think, requires that it be understood and appreciated. Christians, we know, who are equally pious and conscientious in their opinions, may differ on this subject. We love our brethren who dissent from us respecting it. We cheerfully accord to them the right of private judgment. It is man's inalienable birthright, — an unquestionable attribute of intelligent existence. And should these pages fall under the eye of any such, — or any who have doubted whether infant baptism is an ordinance of the gospel, — they are requested kindly and cordially to weigh what may now be offered. Possibly, there are views of the subject which they have not taken, or facts and arguments possessing greater importance than they have supposed. Truth and duty lie on one side or the other of the question now to be considered; and it is certainly important to understand which.

The common belief of those who reject the doctrine of infant baptism, is, that the Christian church was instituted and organized at the commencement of the present dispensation, and that, hence, all its ordinances are to be found in positive New Testament enactments. If they are right in the premises, they are undoubtedly right in the conclusion. But, in our view, they are wrong in the premises, and hence the conclusion is erroneous.

The point, then, which first demands our

attention is, Is the Christian church a continuation of the Jewish church? This question deserves full and careful attention; for, in fact, it is the hinge on which the whole argument turns.

We here take the affirmative, which we think capable of being sustained beyond successful contradiction. But before exhibiting the proofs, it is proper to raise and briefly answer the question, *What is a church?*

We answer: *A church is a company of persons whom God takes into covenant with himself, as his professed servants and worshippers, securing to them certain privileges and blessings.* This was the idea under the former dispensation. Such a community was instituted in the family of Abraham. He was required to separate himself from the world, and be a worshipper and servant of Jehovah. Religious institutions

were to be observed by him and his household, and on condition of obedience, certain
privileges and blessings were secured to
him, some of which were temporal, but the
more important of which were spiritual.
In process of time, a code of laws was
given to his descendants for the regulation
of their civil and religious affairs; a regular priesthood was instituted; and a system of religious instruction, and more of
set and outward formality in religious ordinances and worship, was introduced.
When these laws were propounded to
them from Sinai, they said, " All that the
Lord hath said will we do." (Ex. 19:
8.) To render their engagement to be the
Lord's still more formal and solemn, Moses
wrote the law and ordinances which they
had received on Sinai in a book, which was
termed " the book of the covenant." This
he read in the audience of the people, and

they replied, "All that the Lord hath spoken will we do, and be obedient." To seal this solemn engagement, "Moses took the blood [of sacrifices which had been offered] and sprinkled it on the people, and said, Behold the blood of the covenant which the Lord hath made with you concerning all these words." (Ex. 24: 5–8.) Here was a solemn engagement by which the nation became the professed servants and worshippers of Jehovah. And, toward the close of Moses' life, when a strict adherence to the divine commands and ordinances was enjoined, he said, "This day the Lord thy God hath commanded thee to do these statutes and judgments; thou shalt therefore keep and do them with all thy heart and with all thy soul." He then added, "Thou hast avouched the Lord this day to be thy God, and to walk in his ways, and to keep his statutes, and his commandments, and his judgments, and to hearken unto his voice; and the Lord hath avouched thee this day to be his peculiar people, as he hath promised thee, and that thou shouldest keep all his commandments." (Deut. 26 : 16–18.)

These transactions constituted the people of Israel a church, — an organized body of professed servants and worshippers of Jehovah. And so they are styled in the New Testament. Stephen says of Moses, "This is he that was *in the church* in the wilderness." (Acts 7 : 38.) And Paul, in his epistle to the Hebrews, quotes David, in one of the Psalms, as saying, "I will declare thy name unto my brethren; in the midst of *the church* will I sing praise unto thee." (Hebr. 2 : 12.) And this church, collectively and individually, in view of the relation into which God had thus taken it to himself, was required to be holy, — as really so as the church under the Christian dispensation : — " Sanctify yourselves, therefore, and be ye holy; for I am the Lord your God." — " Ye shall be holy; for I the Lord your God am holy." (Lev. 20 : 7. 19 : 2.)

But, advancing from this point in the history of Israel, to avoid an error, we must distinguish between the church and the nation. By surrounding communities, the nation, as a whole, were regarded as worshippers of Jehovah (just as Christian nations are regarded by heathen as made up of Christians); but nothing is more evident from their history, than that, for the greater part of the time, most of them were not.

From the transactions of God with Abraham, and with his descendents at Sinai, it is obvious, that to have been strictly a member of the Jewish church, one must not only have been circumcised, but have professed to be a worshipper of God, and obedient to his requirements. If an Israelite was not circumcised, he had broken God's covenant, — that is, was not in covenant with God; was not a member of the church. If, having been circumcised, he became an idolater, he was not a worshipper of Jehovah, and hence was not a member of the church; and for his idolatry he was required to be put to death. In completing their national and religious arrangements, certain feasts and other observances were instituted, in which they were to profess their adherence to the worship and service of God. (See Ex. 34: 18–23, and Deut. 26: 1–15.) Those who neglected these were not worshippers of Jehovah, and, strictly speaking, were not members of the church; they did not belong to the company of God's professed people. True, the civil and ecclesiastial laws and institutions of the nation were interwoven with each other, and hence the church and

the nation were intimately connected, —
more so, probably, than in any civil
community since. Still, a portion of the
people were worshippers of Jehovah, and
cleaved to his ordinances, and another
portion were not.   The former were, in reality, the church; the latter did not strictly
belong to it.   Hence Paul says, " They are
not all Israel which are of Israel; neither
because they are the seed of Abraham, are
they all children." (Rom. 9: 6, 7.)   The
church was in the nation; but there were
only a few points in its history in which it
embraced the nation generally.   A few re-
marks hereafter to be made, will further
illustrate this point.

Now it is easy to conceive that the same
body, regulated by the same general principles, but with ordinances and rites accommo-
dated to materially different circumstances,
may exist under different dispensations.

This, we maintain, is the fact. The church, under both dispensations, is the same. This is evident, —

1. *From the language of prophecy.* — The predictions which I shall here introduce, are only a few of the many which might be cited.

In the forty-fourth and forty-fifth chapters of Isaiah, the restoration of the Jews from the Babylonish captivity is foretold, and the prediction asserts, " But Israel shall be saved in the Lord with an everlasting salvation : ye shall not be ashamed nor confounded world without end." (45 : 17.) This could not apply to Israel as a nation, because, as a nation, they have been confounded and ashamed. It must therefore apply to them as a church ; that is, to the church in the nation. And it is a solemn assurance that the Israelitish church should never be reject-ed or destroyed. In the fiftieth and fifty-first chapters, the prophet is addressing explicitly the people of Israel: " Where is the bill of your mother's divorcement." — "Look unto Abraham your father, and to Sarah that bare you." Continuing his address, but referring undeniably to gospel times, he thus commences the fifty-second chapter: " Awake, awake, put on thy strength, O Zion; put on thy beautiful garments, O Jerusalem, the holy city; for henceforth there shall no more come into thee the uncircumcised and the unclean," — an evident prediction, not of the ceasing or destruction of the Jewish church when Messiah came, but of its being purified and continued. In the fifty-fourth chapter, personifying Israel as a desolate woman, the prophet says, " For the Lord hath called thee as a woman forsaken and grieved in spirit, and a wife of youth, when thou wast refused, saith thy God. For a small mo-

ment I have forsaken thee; but in great
mercies will I gather thee. In a little wrath
I hid my face from thee for a moment; but
with everlasting kindness will I have mercy
upon thee, saith the Lord, thy Redeemer."
Mark what follows: *"For this is as the
waters of Noah unto me; for as I have
sworn that the waters of Noah should no
more go over the earth; so have I sworn that
I will not be wroth with thee nor rebuke thee.
For the mountains shall depart, and the hills
be removed; but my kindness shall not depart
from thee, neither shall* THE COVENANT OF MY
PEACE BE REMOVED, *saith the Lord that hath
mercy on thee."* God was wroth with the
nation and rebuked it. He utterly rooted it
up, and destroyed it, and scattered its remaining elements to the four winds. This
assurance, then, applies to the church. For
a time, before the coming of Christ, God
hid his face from it. But its perpetu-

ity and prosperity he here secured with an
oath.   In the fifty-sixth chapter, referring to
gospel times, the prophet says, " The Lord
God, which gathereth the outcasts of Israel,
saith, Yet will I gather others to him, besides those that are gathered unto him ; " —
a plain intimation of the continuance of the
Jewish church, and that the Gentiles were
to be gathered into it.   In the latter part of
the fifty-ninth chapter, the prophet predicts
the coming of Christ : " The Redeemer
shall come to Zion, and unto them that
turn from transgression in Jacob."   He then
breaks out, " Arise, shine ; for thy light is
come, and the glory of the Lord is risen
upon thee."   A body then existing, surely,
was addressed ; and if any think that it was
the nation and not the church, let them notice what follows : " But the Lord shall rise
upon *thee*, and his glory shall be seen upon
thee.   And the Gentiles shall come to thy

light, and kings to the brightness of thy
rising. Lift up thine eyes round about and
see, *they come to thee;* thy sons shall come
from far, and thy daughters shall be nursed
at thy side. Then thou shalt see, and flow
together, and thine heart shall be enlarged;
because the abundance of the sea shall be
converted unto thee, and the forces of the
Gentiles shall come unto thee. — And the
sons of strangers shall build thy walls, and
their kings shall minister unto thee: for in
my wrath I smote thee, but in my favor
have I had mercy on thee. — Therefore thy
gates shall not be shut day or night; that
men may bring unto thee the forces of
the Gentiles, and that their kings may be
brought." All this, as it cannot apply to
the nation, must apply to the church. And
a few verses onward it is said, " Whereas
thou hast been forsaken and hated, so that
no man went through thee, *I will make thee*

an eternal excellency, a joy of many gener-
ations." And then again; *" For the Lord*
shall be thine everlasting light, and the days
of thy mourning shall be ended." — No language could more plainly teach that the
Jewish church was to be continued under
the Christian dispensation.

Other similar predictions could be collect-
ed in great numbers from this book; but I will
introduce only one more. In the sixty-second
chapter, the prophet, looking forward to the
new dispensation, predicts that the church
of God should be called by a new name.
And then, further on, he says, " Go through,
go through the gates, prepare ye the way of
the people [those, who, from other nations,
were to come into the church], cast up, cast
up the high way; gather out the stones; lift
up a standard for the people. Behold *thy*
salvation cometh [He who should save the
Jewish church]; behold his reward is with

him, and his work before him. And thou [the Jewish church addressed — thou] shalt be called, *Sought out, a city not forsaken.*"

It would be easy to add other similar predictions from Jeremiah and the shorter prophets. But these are sufficient. And they certainly show that the Jewish church was not rejected at the coming of Christ and a new one formed.

2. The same appears *from the work which Christ is represented as performing for that church.* The natural meaning of the figure which his forerunner applied to him, when he said, " Whose fan is in his hand, and he will thoroughly purge his floor," is, the cleansing of the Jewish church ; not its destruction. Isaiah, predicting the coming of Christ in the passage, " Unto us a child is born, unto us a son is given," represents the Messiah as sitting "*upon the throne of David, and upon his kingdom,* to order it, and to

establish it with judgment and with justice from henceforth and forever" (Isa. 9 : 7), — meaning, evidently, that he was to defend and perpetuate the Jewish church. In the fifteenth chapter of the Acts, the apostle James, before the first Christian council, speaking of the calling of the Gentiles into the church, and referring to a prophecy of Amos, says, " And to this agree the words of the prophet; as it is written, After this I will return, *and I will build again the tabernacle of David* which is fallen down ; and I will build again the ruins thereof, and I will set it up ; that the residue of men may seek the Lord, and all the Gentiles upon whom my name is called, saith the Lord who doeth these things." The work which Christ performed by extending the blessings of salvation to the Gentiles, and gathering them into the church, is here called, a *building again of the tabernacle of David* — a

figure obviously meaning the revivifying and
enlargement of the Jewish church : — and it
seems to be introduced purposely to guard
us against the error that he intended to
destroy that church and constitute another.
Said Christ to the Scribes and Pharisees,
" Other sheep I have which are not of *this
fold;* them also must I bring ; and they shall
hear my voice, and there shall be one fold
and one shepherd." (John 10 : 16.) Christ
was here speaking of his true church, which,
as we have seen, had existed in the Jewish
nation. And he teaches us that the work
which he came to perform, was, to gather
the Gentiles into it. Said Paul to the
Ephesian Christians: " Wherefore remember, that ye, being in time past Gentiles in
the flesh, were without Christ, being aliens
from the commonwealth of Israel, and
strangers from the covenants of promise : —
but now, in Christ Jesus, ye who sometime

were far off, are made nigh by the blood of
Christ." The obvious import of this passage
is, that the converts at Ephesus, by becoming Christians, had been introduced into the
Jewish church, and had become partakers of
the blessings covenanted to them. And as
the result of his reasoning on this topic,
within a few verses, the apostle comes to
this conclusion : " Now therefore ye are no
more strangers and foreigners, but fellow-
citizens with the saints, and of the household
of God; and are built upon the foundation
of the apostles and prophets, Jesus Christ
himself being the chief corner-stone " ; —
language which strongly implies the unity
of the church under both dispensations.
The same idea was evidently before the
apostle's mind, when, in the next chapter, he
says, " That the Gentiles should be fellow
heirs, and of the same body, and partakers
of his promise in Christ by the gospel."

They were to be fellow heirs with some previously existing body to which God had covenanted blessings capable of being inherited, and were to be partakers in Christ by the gospel of the promises made to that body: and we have already seen with whom the covenant constituting a church was formed.

The work, then, which Christ came to perform for the Jewish church was, to purify and enlarge it, and bring the Gentiles into it.

3. The continuance of the Jewish church appears *from the action of the apostolical council at Jerusalem*, as recorded in the fifteenth chapter of the Acts. That council was called to decide on the question whether the Gentile converts should be circumcised, and keep the ritual law. After free discussion, in which there was some variance of opinion, the negative of the question was unanimously sustained.

Now what was the argument by which that conclusion was reached? Was it that the Jewish church, with all its rites and ceremonies, had been abolished, and a new church established in its stead? If Christ had given such instructions, his disciples must have known it. And here was the time, and this the place, to bring out the fact. This would have covered the whole ground, and settled the question at once. But not a hint of the kind appears. Not the slightest intimation was given that it was the will of Christ that the old church should be regarded as abolished, and a new one formed. The inference is plain: no such thing had been done. Had the fact been otherwise, the calling of that council would have been needless. The apostles might and would have said to the churches they formed, " You have nothing to do with the old establishment; it is all done away;

its rites and observances have ceased; and you are on an entirely new foundation." All trouble had thus been spared.

4. *The continuance of the Jewish church was evidently the argument of Paul in the eleventh of Romans.* He begins with the inquiry, "Hath God cast away his people?" [the Jews.] This he answers with an emphatic negative: "God forbid." He then proceeds to illustrate the truth thus announced. Blindness in part had happened to Israel; they had stumbled and fallen: and, in consequence of this, salvation had come to the Gentiles. The persons thus rejected, he represented as branches broken off from an olive-tree, and the believing Gentiles as engrafted in their stead. Now what did he mean by "the good olive-tree?" Not, surely, the Jewish nation; for, becoming Christians did not incorporate the Gentiles with that. The church, as existing under

the Jewish dispensation, was evidently intended. From this, the *pious* Jews were
not broken off: and among them, the believing Gentiles were grafted in, and partook
" of the root and fatness of the olive-tree "—
because " Abraham's seed, and heirs according to the promise," and inheritors of the
spiritual privileges and blessings covenanted
to him and his posterity. This is obviously
the meaning of the passage.

Should any pretend that the good olive-
tree is Christ, this equally proves the identity of the church under both dispensations,
since the members of both are represented
as being in him. The truly pious are never,
in any age of the world, broken off from
Christ. It is only those who are nominally
such. And those whom the apostle represents as being broken off were nominally in
Christ by being nominally in the church.
But being nominally in Christ now, is being

nominally in the church. On this ground, then, the church is the same under both dispensations, since the same thing constituted membership in the one as in the other.

These are a few of the arguments which prove that the Christian church is a continuation of the Jewish church. I see not how the force of them can be evaded. I see not, indeed, how any one, with this question before him, can read attentively the book of Isaiah, and believe otherwise. Christ, as man, was a member of that church. He was "made under the law" (Gal. 4 : 4) ; and " was a minister of the circumcision." (Rom. 15 : 8.) He submitted to the ordinances of that church ; and endorsed its validity. To the multitude and his disciples he said: " The Scribes and Pharisees sit in Moses' seat. All therefore whatsoever they bid you observe, that observe and do." (Matt. 23 : 2, 3.) There were in it, when he came, some

living members, who "walked in all the
commandments and ordinances of the Lord
blameless," and "waited for the consolation
of Israel." Christ came, as we have seen,
to enlarge and beautify it. The object of
his "being made a curse for us," as Paul
expressly declares, was, "that the blessing
of Abraham might come on the Gentiles
through" him. And here we see how it
was that Abraham became "the father of all
them that believe." It was not because he
was the first believer; for he was not. It
was not because he was a more eminent
saint than such men as Enoch and Elijah;
for we have no reason to regard him as such.
It was because he was constituted the head
of the visible church. It was because the
covenant was made with him which constituted the first regularly organized community of God's worshippers, from which all
others are derived. "He received the sign

of circumcision," (says Paul,) — "that he might be the father of all them that believe," both of Jews and Gentiles; —that is, the head of the visible church. (Rom. 4 : 11.)

Let the truth which has now been before us be a fixed fact in our minds. And let us accustom ourselves to feel and speak of the Jewish church with respect. It was God's church; one which he loved; and for the sake of which he reproved kings; and of which he said, " Every tongue that shall rise against thee in judgment, thou shalt condemn." (Isa. 54: 17.) It was never, as some have styled it, a *legal* church. A legal church among those who have sinned is an impossibility. The Israelites were no more expected to acquire merit before God by religious and other observances, than any person or community now is. The religion of a sinner, to be acceptable to God, in any age of the world, must embrace the same

elements.   And happy will it be for us, if a
portion of the piety and grace which adorn-
ed the worthies of the Jewish church is
ours.

CHAPTER II.

THE church, as we have defined it, is *a company of persons whom God takes into covenant with himself, as his professed servants and worshippers, and to whom he stipulates certain privileges and blessings.* — The covenant which God made with Abraham, by which a church was instituted in his family, is therefore the charter of that church's rights. It specifies what he and the church thus formed might expect from God by virtue of that transaction.

It is, then, an important inquiry (and the more so, since, as we have seen, the church under both dispensations is the same), *What*

*blessings did God promise to Abraham?
What was embraced in the charter of rights
given to the church which was organized
among his descendants?*

The engagement with Abraham included
some temporal things; — such as a numerous posterity, the possession of the land
of Canaan by his posterity, and outward
national prosperity on condition of adhering
to the divine commands. But the more important were spiritual blessings. The first
recorded specification, which was made
when he was called to leave his native
country, was, that he should be a blessing,
and that in him all the families of the earth
should be blessed. (Gen. 12: 2, 3.) This
was a promise of all that grace and favor to
him and his posterity by which this should
be accomplished. Some twenty-five years
afterward, a more formal and solemn engagement was made. " And — the Lord

appeared unto Abraham, and said unto him, I am the Almighty God; walk thou before me, and be thou perfect — and I will establish my covenant between me and thee, and thy seed after thee in their generations, for an everlasting covenant; to be a God unto thee, and to thy seed after thee." (Gen. 17: 1, 7.) This covenant was then sealed by the institution and performance of the rite of circumcision. And of this God said, " it shall be a token of the covenant betwixt me and you " (v. 11). — Afterward God promised him, " In thy seed shall all the nations of the earth be blessed " (Gen. 22: 18); referring, as an apostle informs us, specifically to Christ; and meaning that he should come in the line of Abraham's posterity, and that through him, and the church, of which he is the head and the representative, the world should be blessed.

But the point at which the covenant was

formally announced and sealed, embodies
the grand transaction.   All other things
were virtually embraced in this, and were
only specified as defining some of its partic-
ulars.

When God thus solemnly engaged to
Abraham, "I will be a God to thee;" less
cannot be meant than that God would be
his spiritual father and friend, and fulfil the
high import of that sacred relation by im-
parting to him all needful protection, and
bestowing upon him all needful grace, for
time and eternity.   The promise was an assurance of his acceptance with God as a
penitent believer.   Hence an apostle says,
" He received the seal of circumcision, *a seal
of the righteousness of the faith which he had,
yet being uncircumcised.*" (Rom. 4: 11.)
And the promise made to him in behalf of
his children was the same as that made to
himself.   The same language was used; and

no intimation is given that it is employed in an inferior sense. And, indeed, the holy man would have felt it to be a mockery of his highest desires to have temporal blessings only engaged to his children and posterity, while spiritual blessings were engaged to himself. This could not be; because, as the covenant secured the existence of the church among his descendants, it secured the existence of piety; for, where the church is, there piety must be. The promise, "I will establish my covenant between me and thee, and thy seed after thee, in their generations, for an everlasting covenant; to be a God unto thee, and to thy seed after thee," was an engagement that they should be brought into the same relation to God in which himself stood. It was a promise of the bestowment upon them of saving grace. It could mean nothing less than this. Here, indeed, a condition was involved.

3

Abraham must be faithful.   He must be
simply and sincerely devoted to God.   He
must be a priest of Jehovah in his house,
maintaining the worship of God in it, and
governing his household aright, and instruct-
ing them in the things of God.   And in
proportion to his fidelity in these respects
might he claim the fulfilment of the promise
to his children, in its high spiritual meaning;
and through them to succeeding generations.
It was a promise that God would bless
his efforts, by the bestowment of saving
grace upon his offspring, and so downward
in the line of his posterity.   And hence we
hear God saying of Abraham, " I know him,
that he will command his children and his
household after him, and they shall keep
the right way of the Lord, to do justice
and judgment, that the Lord may bring
upon Abraham that which he hath spoken
of him." (Gen. 18 : 19.)   Such was the

charter of privileges given to the Jewish church.

Another question here arises: *Was this charter revoked or altered at the commencement of the Christian dispensation?* — The fact, already proved, that the church remains the same, is, in itself, presumptive evidence that the charter is not annulled; for, the annulling or withdrawing of a charter, unless a new one is given, dissolves the body which it had created. But, has it ceased to be a law of God's moral administration, through Christ and the church to bless the world? Is it no longer a fact, that God blesses children through their parents? Is not the truth written on every page of the church's history, that the prayers, instructions, and example of pious parents are one of his chosen instrumentalities for the conversion and salvation of their offspring? As well may we expect the laws of nature to cease as that principle to cease, which has run through the whole of God's moral govern-ment of the world, which he expressed to Abraham in the points before us, and which, through him, he solemnly covenanted to the church.

But perhaps it is here said, The Jewish ceremonial law is abolished, and with it went the Abrahamic covenant; — all these Old Testament transactions were swept away. Has the law of the *ten commandments*, then, become null and void? And how came Paul to say that "Christ was a minister of the circumcision for the truth of God, to *confirm the promises made unto the fathers?*" and that "*all the promises of God in him are yea, and in him, Amen,* to the glory of God by us?" (Rom. 15: 8, and 2 Cor. 1: 20.) The ceremonial law, indeed, has ceased; but the covenant with Abraham formed no part of that law. The promise that Christ should come and bless the world, surely, was no part of it. None of the promises made to Abraham were any part of it. They were as distinct from it as any transaction could possibly be. So the apostle reasons in the third chapter of Galatians. "Brethren, I speak after the manner of men: Though it be but a man's covenant, yet if it be confirmed, no man disannulleth or addeth thereunto. Now to Abraham and his seed were the promises made. He saith not, And to seeds, as of many; but as of one, And thy seed, which is Christ. And this I say, that the covenant which was confirmed before of God in Christ, the law, which was four hundred and thirty years after, cannot disannul, that it should make the promise of none effect." The reasoning of the apostle is, that the law, which was given at Sinai 430 years after the covenant made with Abraham, was an entirely distinct thing, and

did not, in the least, affect it. That covenant was confirmed by God in Christ; and,
according to the apostle's showing, being
thus established, could not be disannulled.
It was God's covenant, and hence unspeak-
ably more firm and less mutable than any
human engagement. "The law," he says,
"was added because of transgression, *till
the seed should come* to whom the promise
was made." (v. 19.) It was added [ap-
pended] to the promises made to Abraham
till Christ should come; and then the ceremonial part of it was to be taken away.
The ceremonial law was the "hand-writing
of ordinances" which Christ blotted out and
took away by nailing it to his cross. (Col.
2: 14.) It "was added" and "taken away,"
leaving the Abrahamic covenant just as it
was. That covenant, in all the fulness of
its promises, is still the rich inheritance of
the church. It was never God's design,

under the Christian dispensation, to abridge
the privileges of his people. The very idea,
that, under a better economy, these were to
be diminished, is preposterous. Christ did
not abolish one of the promises made unto
the fathers. He came to confirm and fulfil
them — to fulfil some of them in his own
person, and others in the bestowments of his
spirit and grace. And the apostle, at the
commencement of his argument in the third
of Galatians, is careful to assure us that the
object of Christ's death was, that the blessing
of Abraham might come on the Gentiles.
Christ, he says, "was made a curse for us
— that the blessing of Abraham might come
on the Gentiles through Jesus Christ; — that
we might receive the promise of the spirit
by faith." Justification by faith, and the
Spirit to effect all the blessings, personal and
relative, promised to Abraham, are here announced as coming on the Gentiles through

Christ; and the design of his death was to secure this effect. And hence the conclusion to which the argument of the apostle conducts him : "If ye be Christ's, then are ye Abraham's seed, and heirs according to the promise :" — "heirs" — inheritors of the blessings covenanted to him. The charter of the church, then, remains unchanged.

It has been already remarked that the covenant with Abraham was sealed by the instituting of circumcision. This ordinance was commanded to be strictly observed by all his descendants. And so important did God regard this seal, that he threatened the delinquent with being "cut off from among his people." (Gen. 17: 14.)

But why did God affix a seal to his covenant with Abraham? and why did he consider it so important that its neglect should incur the forfeiture of the subject's life? — for such is probably the meaning of the

threatening. (See Ex. 31: 14.) God's
word of promise, surely, needs no additional
security. His veracity is not to be doubted.
The seal was intended to meet an infirmity
of humanity — to confirm to men God's
fidelity to his engagements, and remind them
of implied obligations and duties. God
knew man's proneness to forget. Even Abraham needed to have his faith in the divine
promises strengthened. And his posterity
would need to be reminded of the solemn
transactions between God and their progenitor; and of the relation into which they
were brought to God, and of what he consequently expected of them. This would
tend to secure them to his service; to reclaim them when they wandered; and to inspire them with confidence in his promises
in seasons of calamity and trial. It was
given to Abraham for the same reason that
a token was given to Noah and the post-

diluvian world, that a flood should not again destroy the earth. It was given on the same principle, that, under the Jewish dispensation, types prefigured blessings to come ; and, under the Christian, ordinances are remembrances and seals of blessings bestowed. Every outward institution is intended to meet some necessity of our nature: and such memorials will be requisite while that nature remains what it has been, and what it is.

If, then, the covenant with Abraham — the great charter of the church's rights — remains, a seal is to be expected. It would be preposterous to suppose that a covenant, once sealed, and still in force, has had its seal removed. When the testimony of validity is removed from an instrument, it becomes void. Unless, therefore, God is less benevolent than he once was — less desirous of human welfare — or man has become more observant of his Maker's will, and needs less reminding; we may be sure that his covenant has still a seal. Can we for a moment admit, that, under the Christian dispensation, faith has less to encourage and strengthen it, less to feed and live upon, than under the Jewish? Can we admit that it has a narrower range of promise, or less security for the fulfilment of divine engagements? Such a supposition would be at war with all the representations of increased advantages under the present economy. It would be little less than a libel on that dispensation itself. Or can any pretend that parents are so much more careful of the religious training of their children as to need less reminding; or that they have so much more confidence in the fulfilment of God's promises than even Abraham had, that they need no encouragement from an outward and impressive rite? Such inquiries need no replies.

But here it may be asked, If the Abrahamic covenant remains, why is not its
original seal continued? I reply : The per-
petuity of that covenant is unaffected by the
question whether or not we can see the reason of the discontinuance of circumcision.
But further; 'that rite, though instituted
long before the giving of ceremonial law,
had come to be regarded as a pledge to fulfil it. Said Paul to the Galatians, " I testi-
fy again to every man that is circumcised,
that he is a debtor to do the whole law."
(Gal. 5: 3.) The Judaizing teachers insist-
ed that unless the Gentile converts were
circumcised and kept the law of Moses, i. e.
the ceremonial law, they could not be saved;
thus subverting the very foundation principle of the gospel, justification by faith
in Christ alone. Hence the sharp conten-
tion which arose respecting this question,
and the calling of the council at Jerusalem

to decide it. If the Gentile converts were circumcised, they would be virtually proselyted to the Jewish religion, and be pledged to all its observances as requisite for acceptance with God. It hence became indispensable that circumcision should be laid aside. If this was not the only way in which the evil could be corrected, it was the readiest way, and the one which the Holy Ghost designated. And it should be specially noticed that this connection between circumcision and the ceremonial law was the sole ground of argument before the council at Jerusalem, and the reason on which its decision was based. The question was not, Circumcision as the seal of the Abrahamic covenant; but, *Circumcision as connected with the Jewish ceremonial law.* And if any should ask why, if that rite as a seal of the covenant had given place to another, nothing was said about the change,

we reply : That nothing was said respecting
this, we do not know.   But this was not the
point at issue ; and, therefore, the brief result
is silent respecting it.   Nor was it needful
to raise that question, since, as we contend,
another rite had been substituted, and was
generally observed.

This leads us to the next point in order :
*Was the form of the seal of the Abrahamic
covenant changed at the introduction of the
gospel dispensation ?* — If no other reason
for such a change had existed but the
Saviour's foresight of the abuse to which
circumcision would be subjected, this was
sufficient.   And, further, it is not unnatural
to expect, that, with the introduction of a
milder dispensation, and one suited to a
more highly civilized state of the world, and
with the ceasing of sacrifices when the great
sacrifice which they prefigured had been offered ; all bloody rites would cease, and a

rite of similar moral significancy would take the place of circumcision. A rite of similar significance existed; and had from time immemorial. Those, who, from other nations, were proselyted to the Jewish religion, were circumcised and baptized, — males submitting to both rites, and females to the latter. The latter rite [baptism] the Saviour adopted as a token of discipleship to him, by commanding it to be applied to all who should embrace the gospel. " Go teach all nations, baptizing them in the name of the Father, and of the Son, and of the Holy Ghost." *He thus placed baptism, as an initiatory rite, in the same relation to the Christian church in which circumcision had stood to the Jewish.* It became a necessary prerequisite to membership. And, to adult receivers, it became *precisely what circumcision was to Abraham,* " *a seal of the righteousness of faith* " — a seal of acceptance and justification by faith.

In emblematic significancy, circumcision
and baptism are precisely similar. The
typical import of circumcision is, the renewal of the heart to holiness — cleansing from
moral defilement. "Circumcise therefore
the foreskin of your heart, and be no more
stiff-necked:" "And the Lord thy God will
circumcise thy heart, and the heart of thy
seed, to love the Lord thy God with all thy
heart, and with all thy soul." (Deut. 10: 16.
30: 6.) And Paul speaks of the Christians at Colosse as "circumcised with the
circumcision made without hands, in putting
off the body of the sins of the flesh." The
typical import of baptism is the same — the
renewal of the heart to holiness — cleansing
from the defilement of sin. Hence the following declarations; "For as many of you
as have been baptized into Christ, have put
on Christ;" — have become morally like
him. (Gal. 3: 27.) "Know ye not that so

many of you as were baptized into Jesus Christ, were baptized into his death:" i. e. have become dead to sin. (Rom. 6 : 3.) The direction of Ananias to Saul expresses the typical import of this rite: " Arise, and be baptized, and wash away thy sins." (Acts 22: 16.) Literal circumcision and literal baptism are emblems of spiritual circumcision and spiritual baptism. But in the following passage, the two latter are placed before us as being precisely similar in nature and effect: " In whom ye are circumcised with the circumcision made without hands, in putting off the body of the sins of the flesh by the circumcision of Christ; buried with him by baptism, wherein also ye are risen with him through the faith of the operation of God, who hath raised him from the dead." (Col. 2 : 11, 12.)

These two rites, then, mean the same thing; and the latter, by Christ's express

4

command, stands in the same relation to the Christian church in which the former did to the Jewish. But we have seen that the church is the continuation of the Jewish church. It follows, then, that by Christ's express command, baptism takes the place of circumcision. It is a token of the same covenant and a seal of the same spiritual blessings. This result has been reached by a process of reasoning which we think is legitimate and conclusive. We see not how any position we have taken can be disproved. And here we might rest the propriety of applying baptism to the children of believers. But a few additional arguments should receive attention; and some objections to the conclusion we have reached deserve to be considered.

CHAPTER III.

TWO OBJECTIONS ANSWERED. — FURTHER ARGU-
MENTS. — THE CONDUCT OF CHRIST AND THE
APOSTLES. — NO COMPLAINTS FROM CONVERTED
JEWS. — TESTIMONY FROM HISTORY.

OUR inference from the foregoing reasoning is, that, unless a limitation has been
introduced, the seal of the covenant should
now be applied as extensively as under the
former dispensation; i. e. to the children of
God's professed people. If the covenant remains unchanged, the seal, in its new form,
should be applied by the same rule as before, unless a different rule has been introduced.

Some pretend that a different rule has
been given — that the doctrine of the New

Testament is, that a person must believe before he is baptized. In support of this, it is said, that the multitude on the day of Pentecost were directed: " Repent and be baptized every one of you in the name of the Lord Jesus ;" " and they that gladly received the word were baptized ;" that Philip required faith in the eunuch as a prerequisite to baptism; and that Lydia, and the jailer, and Saul of Tarsus, believed before they were baptized.

All this is true; but the facts do not touch the question of Infant Baptism at all. This is easily shown. The missionaries to the Sandwich Islands, when those who had been trained in heathenism, gave evidence of piety, required every one of them to be baptized in the name of Christ. And why? Did not those missionaries believe in Infant Baptism? They certainly did. And the fact, that, for a number of years, they required all the adults who professed faith in Christ to be baptized was not, in the least, inconsistent with that belief. The reason is plain: The gospel was then just introduced; and, from the nature of the case, those persons could not have been baptized in their infancy. Just so it was in the case before us. The multitude on the day of Pentecost, the eunuch, Lydia, the jailer, Saul, and others, could not have received baptism, when young, because baptism, as a Christian rite, did not then exist: the gospel dispensation had just commenced. The facts thus adduced to disprove the propriety of applying baptism to infants are *entirely irrelevant.* They have not the most distant bearing on the question. Admit the apostles to have been the firmest believers in this doctrine, and they would have done, in all these cases, precisely as they did.

There may, indeed, be a degree of plausi-

bility in the idea of purging the church by
rejecting infants from the covenant, under
the pretence that retaining them tends to
corrupt it by introducing unconverted members. But we deny that Infant Baptism,
properly understood and practised, has any
such tendency. The rite, as we shall hereafter show, does not constitute them
members; and none are more watchful to
admit only the converted than those who
understandingly practise it. God's method
of purifying the church was not to do it by
reducing the number of his promises. It
was never his intention to recall some of
them, and give to faith a narrower scope of
divine engagements, and less food and encouragement. Such an idea is utterly inconsistent with the declaration that *all* the
promises are " Yea," and "Amen," in Christ,
and should be at once and forever dis-
carded.

In this place it is proper to notice another objection to the idea that baptism takes the place of circumcision. It is, that, on embracing Christianity, those who had been circumcised were required to submit to baptism. To this I reply, There was a specific meaning in baptism, over and above what was implied in circumcision. Circumcision was an acknowledgment of Jehovah as the only true God, and a profession of subjection to him as such in the character of worshippers and servants. Baptism includes all this; and is also a specific profession of discipleship to Christ. It involves a definite acknowledgment that Jesus of Nazareth is the true Messiah, a profession of faith in him as such, and a consecration to his service.* Hence the multitude on the day of

---

* Should any suppose that this remark conflicts with the application of baptism to infants, it is suf-

Pentecost were required to be baptized "*in the name of the Lord Jesus.*" The converts at Samaria also, and Cornelius, and others, are said to have been "*baptized in the name of the Lord Jesus.*" Not that the name of the Trinity was not placed upon them; but that a leading and specific idea was, *a profession of discipleship to Christ.* At the introduction of the new dispensation, it was proper that the rite of initiation, while it had the same emblematic significance as the one which preceded it, should imply more, and hence be required of those who had submitted to the other. Those, generally, who had been circumcised, hated and rejected Christ. It was therefore proper, that, in a specific rite they should be required to acknowledge him

ficient to reply that the baptism of an infant is an act of the parent, and not an act of the child. It implies all this in the parent, and a consecration of his child to Christ.

as the promised Messiah, and engage allegiance to him as their rightful sovereign. This was God's method of purifying the church. By introducing a new test, he virtually broke off the unfruitful branches, and cleansed the church of unworthy members. The believing Jews submitted to Christ, and believing Gentiles were added; and thus, out of twain, upon the previous foundation, was formed a more pure and spiritual body than the previous organization had been.

I now proceed to adduce a few additional arguments in support of the sentiment that Infant Baptism is an ordinance of the gospel.

1. *Christ and his apostles taught and practised just as we should have expected, if children were still to be regarded as in covenant with their parents, and just as we should not have expected on the contrary supposition.* We should bear in mind that

Christ and his apostles belonged to a nation, who, during their whole history, had been taught to dedicate their children to God by a solemn religious rite, and this, because, with their parents, they were entitled to certain specific blessings. These facts were associated with all their ideas of true religion and the principles of the divine administration. In conformity to an express divine injunction, they had been accustomed to see Jewish children receive the token of the covenant made with their early progenitor. When any from among the Gentiles were disposed to embrace their religion, they had seen the children of such families embraced in the covenant transaction by which the parents consecrated themselves to the service of Jehovah. The practice of receiving children with their parents to the blessings of the same covenant, was rooted in their minds as among the fundamental principles of propriety and right.

Now if Christ intended to introduce a
new order of things in this respect, it is obvious that much instruction would have
been requisite to subdue the prejudices, and
modify the opinions of his disciples, and
prepare their minds for so great a change.
But while he severely criticized the abuses
which had crept into that dispensation, and
the principles and practices of the Scribes
and Pharisees, — while he spared nothing
which required rebuke or censure, and while
he carefully taught the disciples the spiritual
nature of his kingdom; we hear him giving
no such instructions, nor even hinting at the
intention of a change. On the contrary, he
encouraged the bringing of children to him
for his blessing, and rebuked those who
would have hindered the practice, and
because Zaccheus himself was a son of
Abraham, pronounced blessings on his family. And after seeing such things in their

Master, and being reproved by him for an unwillingness that children should be brought to him, and hearing him declare that of such were the kingdom of heaven; would the disciples be likely to infer, that, under the Christian dispensation, he intended to exclude children from the covenant with God into which their parents were brought?   And would they not have waited for an order from him to inaugurate a practice exactly the opposite of that in which they had been trained?   And, strong as were their Jewish prejudices, and slow as they were to relinquish the idea of a temporal kingdom, or yield any of the opinions they had cherished; would not such an order, plain and oft repeated, have been needful to induce them to regard and treat children as no longer in covenant with their parents?   Would not such an order have awaked strange thoughts in their minds, and occasioned conversation and discussion, and excited some manifestation of hostility to such an arrangement? But no such direction appears, nor even an intimation that such a change was intended; nor is there anywhere betrayed, in the intercourse of the disciples, a hint that such a direction had been received. *This is just what we should have expected of the Saviour, and thus far of the disciples, if children were still to be considered as objects of God's covenant favor; and just what we should not have expected if they were not.*

Commissioned by their Redeemer, the apostles went forth to propagate his religion. The Spirit, which had been promised to guide them into all truth, had been given. They acted under his guidance. What was their practice in relation to the point before us? To adults, they administered baptism on a profession of their faith. But did they baptize none beside? This question must be answered by carefully examining the history of their proceedings as given us by the pen of inspiration. Paul and Silas went to Philippi, and preached. Lydia was converted. " She was baptized, and her household." But nothing is said of the *conversion* of its members. This, had it taken place, and almost simultaneously with her own, would have been a remarkable occurrence, and far more worthy of being noted, than the circumstance of their baptism. When it is said that the Lord opened *her* heart, why is it not added, "and the hearts of her household," if, indeed, the fact occurred? This is not said. But it is said that they were baptized. Why the record of the less to the omission of the greater? Is it assumed that their conversion is implied in the fact of their baptism? This is assumption without proof. It is begging the question at issue. It is no-where asserted in the New Testament that *none but believers* are to be baptized. As has been before remarked, converts from the Gentiles to the Jewish church were received with their households. And if no counter order had been given, it would have been perfectly natural for Paul and Silas to receive the household of Lydia with herself. All their views of the stability of the covenant made with their fathers would have led to this. Besides, if the whole household of Lydia was converted with herself, she would have been far more likely to rejoice in the wonderful fact, and to speak of it, than simply to refer to her own. And yet she said to the apostles, " If ye have judged *me* to be faithful to the Lord, come into my house, and abide there," — strongly implying that she was the only believer in the family. If all with herself were believers,

the strongest inducement which the apostles
could have had to comply with her invitation was omitted. And this is the more
singular, as she had to "constrain" them
before they consented. To the remark
sometimes adduced as proof that all her
household were believers — "And they [the
apostles] went out of the prison, and enter-
ed into the house of Lydia; and when they
had seen the brethren, and comforted them,
they departed," it is sufficient to reply,
No intimation is given that they saw them
at the house of Lydia, much less that they
belonged to her family. The meaning is
simply, that they saw them before they left
the city. Here, then, is a household baptized by the apostles without any evidence
that any but its head was pious, and where
all the evidence which the Holy Ghost has
seen fit to give us goes against the idea that
any but herself had received the Saviour.

In the same city, Philippi, the jailor, to whose care Paul and Silas were committed, was suddenly converted; and it is said of him that he and all his were baptized straightway. From its being said that the apostles preached "to all that were in his house," and that he "rejoiced, believing in God, with all his house," some maintain that all his household were believers. But the language in the original gives a different idea. One well qualified to judge says: " If there is any ambiguity in this English phrase, there is none in the original. It is certain from the Greek, as every one acquainted with the language must perceive, that the believing and rejoicing here spoken of, being in the *singular number*, can refer to the jailor only." (Pond on Baptism, p. 96, Edition of 1833.) — The commentator Scott says that the word for believed is singular — thus implying that the jailor only

believed, and that his household were baptized on the ground of his faith. Mr. Scott
renders the passage thus, " He [the jailor]
rejoiced through all his house, having believed in God."

Here, then, is evidence which a mind
open to conviction and inquiring after truth
would be slow to disregard, that two households were baptized on the faith of their
heads. The very mentioning, indeed, of the
baptism of households, is strong presumptive
evidence that the apostles believed and
practised infant baptism. The journals of
missionaries who reject this doctrine may
be searched in vain for such records as are
here made respecting the apostles. And
knowing, as my readers do, that evangelical
Christians are divided on this point, were
they to find, in the journal of any missionary, of whose opinion in this respect they
knew nothing, such entries as these : — " A

certain woman, hearing me preach, believed, and I baptized her and her family;" "A
man embraced the Saviour, and I baptized
him and all his," — they would not hesitate
a moment on which side of the line that
divides Christians on this subject to rank
that missionary. Why judge differently of
the apostles and of him? Were not the
apostles inspired men, whose example and
practice every one wishes should correspond
with his own views, the fact of their baptizing households would be deemed good
reason for believing that they practised infant baptism. No one would be likely to
call this in question in the case of any other,
the record of whose proceedings correspond-
ed with the record of theirs. *The account
given us of the apostles is just such as we
should have expected on the supposition that
they practised Infant Baptism, and just such
as we should not have expected if they did
not practise it.*

2. *If children are not to be retained in covenant under the Christian dispensation, we should have heard loud complaints from the converted Jews.* — That the children of God's peculiar people were entitled to covenant blessings with their parents, was a fact which had run along the whole history of the Hebrew nation, and was strongly associated with the religious principles and feelings of every Jewish mind. And every one, at all acquainted with the history of that people, knows that they were peculiarly tenacious of their rites and ceremonies, and strongly opposed to innovation. Multitudes of them believed, and were brought into the Christian church. But conversion to Christianity did not free their minds from their national prejudices. It was extremely difficult for them to indulge the opinion that any change was to take place in the customs in which they had been trained. They

were " zealous of the law," and disposed to enforce its observance on the Gentile converts.

In the new order of things introduced by the gospel dispensation, had the children been stricken out from their covenant relation to God, the change to the Jews would have been great. It would have been an innovation upon their previous habits of thought and feeling to which no Jewish mind would have quietly submitted. A clamor would have been raised, and discussion would have been long and sharp; and much opposition would have been manifested, before a change could have been effected. How is it, then, that we hear not a word of such discussion? How is it that the question is not even raised? When many other things are discussed, and deviations from the ceremonial law were strenuously opposed, by the Jewish converts, how is it

that not a word is said about this? Any
one who can believe that such a change
could have been effected without a syllable
of controversy, must be strangely ignorant
of the strength of Jewish prejudices, or must
strangely overlook them.   The entire silence
of the New Testament on this subject is
evidence, which no unbiased mind will feel
at liberty to disregard, that no such change
occurred at the commencement of the Christian dispensation.

3. *History teaches that Infant Baptism was
universally practised in the churches soon
after the apostolic age.* — I shall trouble
the reader with only a few quotations.
Irenæus, who wrote about sixty-seven years
after the apostles, and who was a disciple
of Polycarp, the disciple of John, says,
" Christ came to save all persons who by
him are regenerated unto God; infants and
little ones, and children and youths, and

older persons." (Wall, Vol. I. p. 25.) The fathers of that day used the term " regener-ate" for " baptize " — thus putting the thing signified for that which denoted it. This was evidently the sense in which Irenæus used the word; for, in relation to Christ's command (Matt. 28: 19), he says, " When Christ gave his apostles the com-mand of *regenerating unto God*, he said, Go teach all nations, *baptizing* them." Jus-tin Martyr (a cotemporary with Irenæus), says of certain persons, " They are regenerat-ed in the same way of regeneration in which we were regenerated; for they are *washed with water* in the name of the Father, the Son, and the Holy Ghost." (Pond, p. 99.) Origen, whose father was a Christian martyr, was a very learned man, and flour-ished about one hundred and ten years after the apostles. He travelled quite extensive-ly, and had the best means of knowing the practice of the churches. He says, " According to the usage of the church, baptism is given to infants." Again he says, " Infants are baptized for the forgiveness of sins;" and again, " The church had a tradition from the apostles to give baptism to infants." (Pond, p. 102.)   In the year 253, about 153 years subsequent to the apostles, a council of sixty-six bishops was convened in Carthage, with the learned Cyprian at its head, — a man, who, with many others of that day, braved the fires of persecution, and finally died a martyr to the religion of Christ.   Fidus addressed a letter to that council, wishing to know whether the baptism of infants should be delayed till the eighth day, according to the law of circumcision, or might be administered at an earlier date.   That council unanimously decided that it was not needful to delay it to that time.   (Milner's Ch.

Hist., Vol. I. p. 320.) No question was raised whether infants should be baptized. This, it seems, no one in that venerable body doubted. The point was only, whether it was requisite to regard the law of circumcision as to the time of administering it. That council decided the question submitted to them in the negative; and the whole case shows the opinion of the fathers respecting baptism's taking the place of circumcision. Augustine, whom Milner styles "the great luminary of the century in which he lived," flourished 288 years after the apostles. (Pond, p. 106.) He says, "The whole church practises infant baptism; it was not instituted by councils, but was always in use." He also says, "That he did not remember ever to have read of any person, whether catholic or heretic, who maintained that baptism ought to be denied to infants." And further, "This the church

has always maintained." (Dwight's Theo.
Vol. IV. p. 336.) Pelagius, who was a cotemporary with Augustine, "was born in
Britain, and had travelled through France,
Italy, Africa Proper, and Egypt to Jerusalem." (Dwight.) He rejected the doctrine
of original sin. Augustine urged against
him the doctrine of infant baptism, inquiring why, if infants were not sinful, they
were baptized. Pelagius, of course, had the
strongest temptation to deny the doctrine
and practice of infant baptism, if he could.
But instead of this, he says, " Baptism ought
to be administered to infants with the
same sacramental words which are used in
the case of adult persons." " Men slander
me, as if I denied the sacrament of baptism to infants." " I never heard of any
one, not even the most impious heretic,
who denied baptism to infants." (Pond,
p. 108.)

The apostles were under the special guidance of the Holy Spirit; and they practised infant baptism, or they did not. There must have been uniformity among them: and they introduced the practice in the churches they instituted; or they did not. Irenæus, the pupil of Polycarp, who had been the disciple of John, must have known what the instructions and practice of the apostles had been; and yet he testifies for infant baptism. So did Origen, Augustine, Pelagius, the council of Carthage, and others whose testimony might be introduced. These witnesses show conclusively that infant baptism was universal in the church soon after the apostolic age. If, then, the apostles did not practise it, a universal change must have taken place soon after their time. This could not have been effected without much discussion. Multitudes must have seen the innovation; and many would have lifted their voices against it. Human nature must have been far more pliant then than now, if much warm and angry disputing had not occurred. How is it, then, that not a syllable of this reaches us on the page of history? How is it, that, when other schisms and disputes existed, and the record of them is preserved, not a word is said about this? How is it, that in a council of sixty-six learned and pious bishops, only a century and a half after the apostles, no one lifted his voice against a practice which must have been known to be against apostolic instructions and usage, if the apostles did not believe and practise infant baptism? And how is it that such men as Origen and Pelagius NEVER HEARD, not simply of any church, but of *any individual*, who denied the propriety of infant baptism? If these are reliable testimonies (and we are not aware that any attempt has ever been made to disprove them), the inference is unavoidable, that the apostles taught and practised infant baptism.*

I close this point of the argument by a quotation from the late learned Dr. Dwight. " A person who employed himself extensively in examining this subject, gives the following result of all his inquiries. First. During the first 400 years from the formation of the Christian church, Tertullian only urged the delay of baptism to infants, and that only in some cases; and Gregory only

---

* Infant baptism has been denied to exist in the early ages of the church, and arguments have been employed to sustain the denial. The testimony of these fathers has been *ignored ;* but I am not aware of any attempt to *disprove* it. It stands on the page of history ; and there it will stand, an unanswerable proof of the usage of the churches which the apostles and their successors planted.

delayed it, perhaps, to his own children. But neither any society of men, nor any individual, denied the lawfulness of baptizing infants. — Secondly. In the next 700 years, there was not a society nor an individual who even pleaded for this delay; much less any who denied the right or the duty of infant baptism. — Thirdly. In the year 1120, one sect of the Waldenses declared against the baptism of infants, because they supposed them incapable of salvation. But the main body of that people rejected the opinion as heretical; and the sect which held it soon came to nothing. — Fourthly. The next appearance of this opinion was in the year 1522." He adds: "Had the baptism of infants ever been discontinued by the church, or had it been introduced in any age subsequent to that of the apostles, these things could not have been, nor could the history of them been found." (Vol. IV. p. 337.)

Let us now glance at the points which have been proved, — and proved, we think, beyond the power of successful refutation : — The Christian church is a continuation of the Jewish church ; — The charter of the church's privileges was not annulled or altered at the commencement of the Christian dispensation, — it embraced children before, and it embraces them still ; — At the change of dispensations, baptism, as the seal of the covenant, succeeded to circumcision ; — We hence need no special command to baptize infants — the command, " Go teach all nations, baptizing them in the name of the Father, the Son, and the Holy Ghost," since no qualification or restriction was introduced, involves the duty. We have seen that Christ and his apostles acted just as we should have expected them to act if they believed that children were still to be regarded as embraced in the covenant made with

their parents, and were to receive the seal
of that covenant; — That the rejection of
children would have produced loud complaints from the converted Jews, whereas
not a whisper of such complaint appears ;—
and, That history shows the universal practice of infant baptism in the churches soon
after the apostolic age.

What more proof do we want that Infant
Baptism is an ordinance of the gospel?
What more can any reasonable person ask?
We hope, then, to be excused from the
charge of bigotry or undue positiveness
while we express the feeling that the doctrine
rests on the sure foundation of the word of
God, and will there remain, unmoved by all
the power which may be arrayed against it.

CHAPTER IV.

HAVING, as we think, fairly and conclusively established the doctrine of Infant Baptism, the question naturally arises, " What is the relation of baptized children to the church ? " Are they strictly and properly members, entitled to its peculiar ordinances and privileges ? Since, in establishing this doctrine, we reason from the former dispensation, it may be thought

6

that, without any other qualification, they
should come to the Lord's table.   To this
I reply, that analogy, which, at first sight,
may be thought to lead to this conclusion,
sustains the opposite.   It has been already
shown that the Jewish church was not strictly national, and that only at a few points in
its history did it embrace the entire nation.
Something more than circumcision was requisite to constitute a member of that church.
A person must be — and, by his own act,
he must profess to be — a worshipper of
Jehovah.   All Jewish males were required
to attend the three great national feasts, and
there present offerings to God, and worship.
(See Deut. 16: 16. 26: 10.)   Obedience
to this requirement was a practical personal
profession that one was a worshipper and
servant of Jehovah.   If he refused thus to
do, he virtually separated himself from the
company of God's worshippers, or rather,

did not join himself to it — was not in form or in fact, truly and strictly a member of that church. The passover, it will be remembered, was one of those feasts, and was forbidden to be eaten at any place except at the tabernacle or temple. The injunction was, " Thou mayest not sacrifice the passover within any of thy gates which the Lord thy God giveth thee ; but at the place which the Lord thy God shall choose to place his name in, there thou shalt sacrifice the passover." (Deut. 16 : 5, 6.) Those who did not go up to the feasts, and profess themselves the worshippers of Jehovah, were thus forbidden to eat it. The practical profession of being his worshippers must be made by going up to the feast, before the privilege could be enjoyed. — St. Luke says that Christ went up to the passover at Jerusalem, with his parents, when he was twelve years old, " after the custom of the

feast." (Luke 2: 41, 42.) And the state-
ment of commentators, such as Calvin, Bp.
Patrick, Poole, Rosenmuller, and others, is,
that children at the age of twelve years were
brought by their parents to the temple; and
from that time, they began to eat the passover and other sacrifices. Bloomfield says:
" The custom was, not to take them to the
passover, until they should have attained
the age of puberty, a period which the Rab-
bins tell us was fixed at the twelfth year,
when they were held amenable to the law,
and were called sons of precept. They
were then also introduced into the church,
initiated into its doctrines and ceremonies,
and consequently were taken, with their
relatives, to Jerusalem at the festivals." Dr.
Gill, a learned Baptist commentator, says
(on Luke 2: 42): " According to the maxims
of the Jews, persons were not obliged to the
duties of the law, or subject to the penalties

of it in case of non-performance, until they were, a female, at the age of twelve years and one day, and a male, at the age of thirteen years and one day." He adds, as his own comment on the passage : " They were not properly under the law until they arrived at that age; nor were they reckoned adult church-members till then, nor then neither, unless worthy persons : for so it is said, ' he that is worthy, at thirteen years of age, is called a son of the congregations,' that is, a member of the church."

We see, then, to what conclusion the argument from analogy conducts us. There is no rule which entitles baptized children to the peculiar privileges and ordinances of the church, till they publicly profess faith in Christ. They are brought only within the outer enclosure of the church, and, through the covenanted mercies of God, are peculiarly its hope.

We now proceed to another topic, — The utility of Infant Baptism. Every divinely instituted ordinance is founded upon principles of our nature which created a necessity for its existence, and render it, when rightly understood and practised, highly beneficial. This, we think, is eminently true of the ordinance we are now considering.

It is scarcely needful to premise, that an important part of the Divine plan is to perpetuate and promote religion in the world by means of parental instruction and influence. Every reader of the Bible must be aware of this. Numerous injunctions, both in the Old and New Testament, teach the important truth. The fact, too, is written upon the very constitution of our natures. In our younger years, we instinctively cherish feelings of respect toward those who surround us with the arms of parental affection

and kindness. We look to them for instruction and guidance; and our plastic natures
are moulded materially by their agency
upon us. The principles which they instil
sink deep in our memories, and outlive
many subsequent impressions. The effects
of our early training remain with us, and
generally do more than any other cause, and,
probably, more than all other causes, to
frame our characters, and point out, like the
finger of an index, our future and final des-
tinies.

The parental relation was instituted, and
the affections it involves bestowed, — not
that the body simply, nor yet the mind in
its temporal relations, should be the chief
object of solicitude and care, — but that solicitude for the welfare of the undying spirit
should be cherished, and that the instruction
should be given, and the influence exerted,
which, with the blessing of God, will cause

the principles of holiness to spring up within, and advance in strength to the government and sanctification of the soul, and to
its ultimate perfection and felicity in heaven.

And here, as in every other undertaking,
success will, in general, be proportioned to
the diligence and faithfulness with which
the means are employed.   The parent who
feels his responsibility, and labors and prays
to be qualified to meet it, and carefully and
diligently imparts instruction to his tender
charge, and fervently seeks the Divine blessing upon them, and accompanies his efforts
with a godly example in other respects, will
be instrumental of their salvation.   He is
sowing seed in a susceptible soil; and, as
surely as the husbandman reaps a harvest
as the result of his toil, will a rich harvest
unto eternal life be realized from the germs
of truth and holiness which he deposits.
He shall ultimately appear before the throne

of God, with unspeakable joy, surrounded
by those for whom he has toiled and wept.
On the contrary, if he is negligent, his offspring may rise into life without those impressions of truth which their state and necessities require, may pass through the years
allotted them on earth without religion, and
may be found on the left hand at the day
of final account. This is as certain as that
the neglect of means in any other department of the divine government will result in
the failure of the ends which means are intended to secure. Means and ends, in the
government of God, have a sure connection.
And they are no more surely connected in
any other department than in the moral and
spiritual. Here it is more certain than in
any other, that "whatsoever a man soweth,
that shall he also reap."

It follows, that whatever tends to promote
faithfulness in the religious education of

children, tends to their salvation and to the
promotion of piety in the world. Here,
then, is my first argument for the utility of
the doctrine and practice of Infant Baptism : —

*It tends to increase parental faithfulness in
the religious instruction and training of children.*

No man is so ignorant of the principles of
our nature as entirely to discard the use of
forms. In pecuniary affairs, why is a
promise or a note better than a simple
purpose of the mind? and why is a written
agreement better than a mere understanding? An important part of the benefit is,
that the act of thus formally binding in-
creases a sense of obligation.

On this principle — the usefulness of
forms — God has dealt largely with our
race from the beginning. The patriarchs
and the Israelites were more likely to feel

their guilt and their desert at the divine
hand when they saw the sacrifice offered to
expiate their guilt, first bleeding and then
smoking upon the altar, than if no such rite
had been instituted. The Jewish parent, as
he saw the painful ceremony which the law
required, administered to his child, would
be more likely to feel, than he otherwise
would have been, that that child possessed
a corrupt nature, which needed to be taken
away, and corrupt passions and affections
which it might cost painful effort to mortify
and exterminate. So, under the Christian
dispensation, the ordinance of the Supper
was instituted, and attendance on it required, because the solemnity of the service
tends to bring near to the mind, and impress
on the heart, the important truths which
cluster round the cross of the expiring Saviour. One reason, why the act of outward-
ly and solemnly covenanting with God in a

public profession of religion is a duty, is, that it tends to impress on the mind one's obligations to be God's, and to live for him in the world. The outward offering of prayer is better than the mere desires of the heart, because it tends to fix the thoughts and add intensity to the desires. Public worship is a duty, because its several forms tend to beget and foster in the soul the feelings of devotion. And he who fancies that one may be just as good a Christian without outward forms — without prayer, without public worship, without open profession and attendance on special ordinances — as with them, is astonishingly ignorant or careless or perverse. He applies a principle in the high concerns of religion which he knows to be unsound, and which he would not trust in any other department.

On the same ground of utility, which underlies other religious ordinances, do we maintain that Infant Baptism is impressively significant and highly salutary. In this rite, the parent is solemnly reminded that in his child (so young, perhaps, as to be almost unconscious of its own existence), are wrapped the germs of immortality, that these will be developed and matured, and that heaven or hell will be the certain and amazing issue of its individual being. He is reminded of the pollution of its nature, — that from its earliest infancy it needs cleansing, and must have it, or never be admitted to heaven. He is reminded that the little creature whose very being twines so strongly around his heart is not his, but God's, — that his Creator claims it as his own peculiar property, and commits it to him to be cared for and trained with special reference to his service and kingdom both here and hereafter. He is thus reminded of his solemn responsibility — that if he is faithful in prayer and effort — if he guides and guards and instructs, and pleads for, his now helpless offspring as he should, its usefulness and blessedness will be the happy result; and if he is negligent, disaster and ruin, here and hereafter, may be the consequence. He is also reminded of God's promised aid to his endeavors, and the certainty of success, if his efforts are made in humble and persevering faith.

Fix your eye, then, upon a parent who has recently received the precious gift of a "second self." See him bringing this object of his tenderest affection into the house of God, before a solemn assembly of worshippers, that he may consecrate it to the Lord and Saviour to whom he has given himself. The solemnity of the duty presupposes the existence of thought and prayer respecting his obligations, and the necessities and destiny of his child. He brings it

and devotes it to God, and prays for its acceptance, and for the bestowment upon it of
the purifying influences of the Spirit so impressively signified by the ordinance administered. He enters into solemn covenant
with God respecting that child. He pledges
himself, there, in the presence of God and
his people, to train and educate that child
for Christ, — that the instructions he gives
in any thing useful, and the privileges and
advantages he procures for it, shall be with
the express design of fitting it to be a good
and useful subject of His kingdom. He
pledges his own daily, humble, earnest, persevering prayers to God in its behalf, and
that he will store its opening mind with
divine truth, and surround it with motives
to godliness. And he takes hold of God's
covenant engagements to bless his efforts
and save his child.

Now we ask, will all this have no good

effect upon a Christian parent's heart? Can
he have distinctly placed before his mind,
and pressed upon his heart, all the solemn
truths and facts involved in this ordinance,
and pass from such a scene with no increased impression of the state and necessities
of his child, and his own responsibilities and
duties? Will he be moved to no more ear-
nestness of prayer by having an ordinance
indicative of its true relation to the government of God, placed, as it were, at the very
threshold of its being? Will he be stimulat-
ed to no more diligence of effort by thus
seeing how much depends on him, and what
he has solemnly engaged to do? And will
his faith derive no encouragement and
strength from God's promised assistance,
assured to him in the covenant of which he
has taken hold? To say that all this is useless, is to contradict some of the plainest
principles of our nature. It is not useless.

When properly understood and performed, it cannot be. The parent, who, with a right apprehension of the nature of the transaction, and with true piety of feeling and purpose, thus consecrates his child, is benefited himself by being brought into a closer covenant relation to God, and by being rendered more faithful in duty; and the richest blessings will result to the precious object of his affection and solicitude. And to object to the utility of this ordinance by saying that the happy results, as here indicated, are seldom, if ever, fully seen, would be just as valid as to object against the Lord's supper by saying that it exerts not all the influence on Christian hearts and lives which it should. The very fact that there is ground for such an objection against Infant Baptism, shows the necessity of such an institution. It shows that parents need all the helps to faith and duty which the ordinance

involves. At best, they are apt to be forget-
ful and negligent. At best, too many of
their children perish through their neglect.
God foresaw the necessities of the case, and,
in mercy to them and their offspring, instituted an ordinance most happily calculated
to help their infirmities, and lead to blessed
results.

2. Infant Baptism tends to procure for
children the prayers and pious co-operation
of the church. Few things are more solemn
and impressive than to see a little infant,
scarcely conscious of its own existence, publicly presented to God in this ordinance,
and then to have the prayers of the whole
congregation centred on the spiritual and
immortal welfare of that tender and beautiful object. Who that has any sense of the
worth and importance of religion, or any
belief in God as a hearer of prayer, would
not value an interest in such supplications

in behalf of his own children? Any Christian, surely, has few parental sympathies whose heart is not warm, and his supplications fervent, on such an occasion. And the ear of Him who said, " Suffer the little children to come unto me, and forbid them not," must be open to such requests. Few petitions accord better with the tenderness of his nature as thus expressed, or are more sure to receive answers of peace.

But the influence of infant dedication ends not with the act or the hour of its performance. That which tends to strengthen the faith, and encourage the hope, and stimulate the effort, of individual parents, is a blessing to the church as a whole. And we hazard nothing in saying that those churches which place the highest and most enlightened estimate on Infant Baptism, pray most, and most fervently, for the children of the church. They view the offspring

of the household of faith as standing in a
covenant relation to God and the church,
and the body as being the depositary of
promises and blessings in their behalf, and
as sustaining an important responsibility
respecting their character and destiny. If
they see such children entering the paths of
vice or error, they feel an additional inducement, and a stronger obligation, to admon-
ish and save them from ruin. The con-
sciences of children, too, by proper instruction may be made to feel that the fact of
having been consecrated to God is inconsistent with indulgence in carelessness, folly,
and sin ; and imposes upon them increased
obligation to second the wishes of their
pious and anxious parents by consecrating
themselves to Christ. And we believe that
the time is coming when Christians will
better understand, and more deeply feel, the
duties and obligations involved in infant

dedication, and will be more faithful to Christ and his cause in this respect; and that, as a consequence, children will be converted while young; and that thus the glorious period will be introduced when "all shall know the Lord from the least to the greatest."

3. The act of giving children to God in baptism tends to soothe a parent's heart, if called to lay them in an early grave. Many a father and mother, as they have stood by the bedside of a dying child, have been quieted into sweet submission to the divine will, by remembering the consecration of it to God which they made in baptism. They then surrendered it to him, as its Creator and Sovereign; and it is his. Strong as may have been their desires for its recovery, they have felt that it belonged not to them to dictate whether he should restore or remove it. They have keenly felt the rod,

but have kissed it, and bowed, and from the heart have said, " Thy will be done."

The writer here speaks from experience. In troubles of this kind (and often has the bitter cup been put into his hand — and he cannot pen this remark without pausing for a tear over recollections of the past), he has experienced consolation from the fact of having given his children to God in baptism. At such times he has felt that the ordinance *is a blessed privilege.* When he has looked on a dying child, it has calmed an almost bursting heart to remember that the child *was not his* — that he *did surrender it to God in that specific and solemn act.* Thousands of parents have felt the same. Rightly understood and practised, the act of dedicating children to God is full of heavenly consolation. It is fraught with many advantages while children live; it yields sweet peace and comfort if they die. Eternity alone can unfold what benefits it has conferred on parents; and how many children, by the influences it involves, have been rescued from sin, and raised to the felicities and honors of heaven.

Such are some of the benefits of Infant Baptism. It is infinitely too sacred and important ever to be treated with lightness. Every Christian parent should cleave to it, as of inestimable value; and he should pray for grace to realize upon himself and his offspring the fulness of its blessings.

The eyes of some, who have thus consecrated their children to God, will fall on these pages. That act, my friends, was only the commencement of your duty. In a solemn covenant transaction, you gave them to God, and solemnly pledged yourselves to a faithful endeavor to train them for Him. Think often of the engagement which you bound upon your souls, and how much it

constantly requires of you. Think much of
the consequences connected with fidelity or
neglect. God is faithful to his promises;
and you may expect success, if you address
yourselves, humbly and earnestly, to your
work. The prospect of success should fire
your hearts and inspire your endeavors; for,
what greater blessedness can you have than
to appear before the throne at length, surrounded by the objects of your tenderest affection. Thousands of children will bless
God forever for the prayers and faithfulness
of their parents. How delightful the thought
that yours — all of them — may be of this
happy number. Labor and pray, with
constant and tearful assiduity, that so it
may be. The blessedness of the result will
more than repay all your anxiety and toil.

Multitudes of children will find their portion with "hypocrites and unbelievers," because the unfaithfulness of their parents

suffers them to perish in their sins. The hallowed paternal influences, which would reclaim and save them, are wanting; and they go down to the abodes of darkness as the natural result of their own transgressions. Many of these, it is feared, will go from the families of professedly pious parents. Many more will go from families whose heads are not pious. Do I address any parents of the latter class? I pray you, respected friends, to remember that the same great duties grow out of the relations subsisting between you and your children, as result from those existing between the religious and their offspring. The same consequences, also, are connected with fidelity or neglect. Slumber not over the pressing necessities of your offspring. Their souls are infinitely precious; and the same agencies and influences are requisite for their salvation as are needful for that of others. If

you have any care for their immortal welfare, give yourselves to Christ, and com-
mence the labor you have too long neglected. The connection between you and your
children will be endless in its consequences.
Oh, think of this. Ponder it well. There
is no escaping from the solemn fact. Awake,
then, to your own necessities and theirs.
Pray for them. Pray with them. Instruct
and exhort them, and do what you can to
bring them to Christ. God may bless the
effort, and give you cause of everlasting
joy.

Many of the dear children who constitute
our Sabbath Schools are the subjects of
pious parental solicitude and care. Not a
few of you, young friends, have been devoted to God in that solemn rite which we
have now considered. Have you devoted
yourselves? Should you not? What more
reasonable than that those who have receiv-

ed so many instructions, and for whom so many prayers have been offered, should give the morning of their days to Christ? God has brought you into a peculiar relation to himself and his church, and surrounded you with many influences to draw you toward himself and heaven. Yield to their sweetly constraining power, and give your hearts to Him who died to cleanse them with his blood.

There is no more beautiful sight on earth than to see the young turning to the Lord. And if any of you have not pious parents to feel and labor for your good, the Saviour's arms are, notwithstanding, open to receive you. To you, his invitation is, "come unto me, and I will cleanse and guide and save you." There is room enough in heaven for you. There angels wait to rejoice over your repentance, and to welcome you among the followers of the Lamb. If your parents

pray not for you, pray the more earnestly
for yourselves. If they care not for your
souls, you should feel the deeper solicitude,
and exercise the greater care yourselves.
We know not how many may have felt
their way alone to heaven. May the Lord
enable you to reach that happy place!

E N D.